KB005873

Journalism as Resistance

: A History of Struggle for Press Freedom in Korea

Journalism as Resistance:

A History of Struggle for Press Freedom in Korea

Publisher : Korea Foundatidn for Press Freedom
Tel +82-2-6101-1024 Fax +82-2-6101-1025
www.kopf.kr
Printed : September 2019
Design : DesignCursor
Translated : Hangil Jang
ISBN : 978-89-

Journalism as Resistance

: A History of Struggle for Press Freedom in Korea

Korea Foundatidn for Press Freedom

History of Journalism in Korea

: Dishonor and Resistance

Not much pride or honor may be attributed to the history of journalism in Korea. In fact, it is painfully ridden with dishonor and hypocrisy, as the press, supposedly the closest ally of democracy, has collaborated with the authoritarian regimes and turned its back on democracy.

While collaborating with the authoritarian regimes, the post-Liberation press of Korea has interfered with the reunification efforts, closed their eyes to various infringements on the freedom of speech and thought, and remained silent when faced with the human rights violations and the death of many innocent citizens.

In the course of such humiliating history, upstanding journalists who kept both faith in the freedom of the press and responsibility toward its defense have resisted. While approximately a thousand of these journalists were forcibly laid off from their work and sometimes even put to death by the authoritarian regimes and their press collaborators, they persistently kept the precious fire of democracy alive and were able to pass it on in today's society.

Although today's civil society allows no room for the remnants of the past authoritarian regimes to thrive again, the forces of capitalism is becoming ever more intricate and extensively structured, tightening its grip on the freedom of the press. However, the situation is not as bleak as it seems, as the solidarity between upstanding journalists and social activist groups is getting stronger.

The purpose of this small booklet is to inform today's

readers of the presence of journalism in Korea and its challenges, serve as a historical record of the struggles of Korean journalists, and seek solidarity with overseas organizations whose faith in democracy aligns with ours. Buyoung Lee, the chairman of the board of Korea Foundation for Press Freedom (Chayuŏllon Silch'ŏnjaedan), first proposed the idea for this booklet, and it materialized through writings of Rae Boo Park, Sook Lyol Ryu, Wan Kee Lee (lead author), Gangho Park, and Myung Jai Lee.

Against the history of hypocrisy and widespread pretentiousness, we hope to see a tradition and philosophy of fair and impartial journalism prevail. We would also like to pay deep respect to our senior journalists who stood their ground to the very end on the road to democracy.

On behalf of the contributors,

Rae Boo Park

October 2019

Content

Journalism as Resistance
: A History of Struggle for Press Freedom in Korea

Introduction:

One Hundred Years of Domination, Control, and Resistance in Korean Journalism

By the virtue of its role as society's watchdog that reports on the public opinion and the current of the times, journalism carries an activist aspect. However, journalism also regresses from time to time when the press colludes with, is ruled by, or itself becomes those in power. Thus, in any era, it is possible to witness journalism serving as a form of initiative that seeks to reform and rectify the distorted press conditions.

In the late Chosŏn period, the role of journalism amounted to social enlightenment. Although the government news outlet and the private newspapers at the time had different views on the realities of Korean society, all of them insisted on political autonomy, enlightenment, and "self-strengthening." However, these nationalist news outlets were eliminated shortly before and in the wake of the Japan–Korea Annexation Treaty of 1910.

The March 1st Movement of 1919 was a historical turning point where Korean people fundamentally refused Japan's colonial rule and resolved to restore national sovereignty and democracy. The protest for Korea's independence continued for months, and thousands lost their lives at the protest sites and prisons. Underground newspapers like *Chosŏn tongnipsinmun* (*The Chosŏn Independent*) began to circulate, expressing their will and the necessity of independence. These newspapers marked the beginning of the century-long history of journalism as resistance in Korea.

The March 1st Movement resulted in the transition of Japan's colonial policy from the Military Rule (*budan seiji*) to the Cultural Rule (*bunka seiji*), which sought to undermine Korea's ethnic integrity by intensifying its "spiritual domination" over Koreans. While taking advantage of what was at stake for the Korean plantation owners and capitalists, the colonial government cunningly justified their rule under the disguise of cultural nationalism (*munhwaminjokchuŭi*) and "ability fostering theory" (*sillyŏkyangsŏngnon*) via newspapers like *Dong-A Ilbo* and *Chosun Ilbo*, both of which were founded during this period. Sin Ch'aeho, who insisted on organizing mass protests and "the righteous army" (*ŭibyŏng*), criticized the cultural nationalism in his "Declaration of Chosŏn Revolution" (Chosŏn hyŏngmyŏng sŏnŏn): "When a nation is deprived of its right to life under the system of economic exploitation, the very preservation of its people will be called into question, let alone the possibility of their cultural development."

It was progressive newspapers with socialist leanings that led anti-colonial and reunification movements throughout the Japanese colonial rule, the U.S. military occupation and the dictatorship of the authoritarian regimes. However, those newspapers either were targeted and shut down by the ruling regimes of their era or closed down due to lack of funding. In 1927, the colonial government pressured *Chosun Ilbo* into firing a group of journalists who were anti-Japan socialists. In the immediate aftermath of Liberation in 1945, when freedom of the press was supposedly everywhere, socialist newspapers were singled out and removed by the U.S. military government, which promoted anti-communism as the most important political agenda in the peninsula. *Minjogilbo* (*Nation Daily*), whose reunificatory effort and peace activities were remarkable, was shut down under Park Chung-hee's military dictatorship in 1961, only a year after the April 19 Revolution. The decline of socialist newspapers also resulted in the conservative corporate media's monopoly over the newspaper market and their perpetuation of extreme cold war logic even to this date.

More than a decade later, the *Dong-A Ilbo and Chosun Ilbo* journalists who opposed Park Chung-hee's authoritarian rule penned "Declaration of Undertaking Freedom of the Press" (Chayuŏllon silch'ŏn sŏnŏn) in 1974, which marked one of the first organized struggles among journalists. These journalists who were removed from Dong-A and Chosun formed Dong-A Committee of Press Freedom Protection (Tonga chayuŏllon suhot'ujaeng wiwŏnhoe; Tonga t'uwi in short) and Chosun Committee of Press Freedom Protection (Chosŏn chayuŏllon suhot'u-jaeng wiwŏnhoe; Chosŏn t'uwi in short), and continued their fight. Even to this date, one hundred and thirteen Dong-A Committee journalists who were dismissed at the time have been carrying on their mission for the freedom of the press for over forty-five years.

In 1980, Chun Doo-hwan overtook the power after a coup and the Gwangju Massacre, and began controlling the press by enforcing censorship and press policies that forcibly laid off journalists who were even willing to risk going on strike in their resistance. The dismissed journalists subsequently organized the Association of the Dismissed Journalists of 1980 (80nyŏn hae-jigŏllonin hyŏbŭihoe) and carried on their protest against the Chun Doo-hwan regime's oppressive press control.

The dismissed journalists in the 1970s and 80s were foundational figures and a huge asset for the struggle for freedom of the press in Korea. In order to protest against the military dictatorship and its control of the press, journalists from the Dong-A Committee and the Chosun Committee, the dismissed journalists in the 80s, and publishers with social awareness coalesced into Democratic Press Movement Association (Minjuŏllon undong hyŏbŭihoe; Ŏnhyŏp in short) in 1984 and launched an organized struggle. Through the Democratic Press Movement Association's publication *Mal* ("words"), the journalists exposed the brutality of the Chun Doo-hwan regime and the reality of press control, which was evidenced by the government enforcement of the so-called "reporting guidelines." Their effort finally came to bear fruit with the June Democratic Uprising in 1987.

The Korean society ushered in procedural democracy after the June 1987 uprising. Gone were the forms of physical violence including assault, unlawful arrest, and torture, which were imposed frequently on journalists prior to the democratization. Intelligence officials who frequented the news companies were no longer there. Bolstered by the June Democratic Uprising, the press workers organized unions and called for change under the slogans like "press independence" and "internal freedom". Furthermore, the year 1988 witnessed the foundation of the daily newspaper *Hankyoreh*, paving the way for the emergence of progressive media.

The political landscape, however, fluctuated significantly with the birth of a gigantic conservative party through the "three-party coalition" (*samdang yahap*) in 1990, giving rise to a reactionary backlash. Government cronies were parachuted into important positions within the public broadcast companies, and the state mobilized the police force to seize the public media. Against these unfavorable circumstances, the press workers who were already fighting against various forms of media control found ways to secure editorial rights and resist the repression through various programs.

Around this time, the problem of capital as a mode of power also became an important issue, as it began to exert tremendous influence on journalism. In addition to the evils of corporate media and news conglomerates, political lobbying and media sponsorship empowered the capital, which became more fundamental and permanent than the political authority, posing a difficult challenge for those who struggled for freedom of the press.

The ten years of progressive governments, headed by President Kim Dae-jung and then Roh Moo-hyun, began in 1998, providing the basis for both media independence from the state and fair and impartial journalism. With this newly acquired freedom, the press rectified the modern and contemporary history of Korea and investigated into the truth of the purported cases of spy activities and national emergencies that turned out to be rigged by the past authoritarian regimes. Critical exchanges among different media outlets put an end to the "cartel of silence." On the other hand, the conservative media and news conglomerates became ever more reactionary. Even their unions fell subservient to the corporate interests, whereby the initial spirit of fair and impartial journalism became increasingly nominal.

The year 2008 marked the beginning of the conservative governments led first by Lee Myung-bak and then by Park Geun-hye, whose control of the press had become far more institutionalized. The conservative news conglomerate monopolized the newspaper market and became entitled to run commercial broadcast service. The public broadcast's function as a government watchdog weakened and regressed again to pro-government sycophancy. With the fairness and accuracy in reporting set back by decades, an "uneven field" full of conservatives was created. The nine years of conservative governments were full of turmoil, with a series of corruption, lies, and absurd policies. As the news conglomerates and media rushed to defend the government, the media workers went on a mass-scale strike, which corresponded to a series of nation-wide candlelight marches that led to the revolutionary event of President Park's impeachment.

Korea's progressive media was able to develop with the sacrifice of journalists who protested vigorously against the authoritarian regimes and the colluding media conglomerates' employment of media takeover, control, and public opinion rigging, and their legacy continues to resonate to this date.

Cho Yongsu and *Minjogilbo*'s
Revolutionary Journalism

The ethos of March 1st Movement of 1919 was still alive among Korean journalists after the liberation of Korea. These journalists resisted against the unjust power under the slogans of political autonomy, reunification, and democracy. On the contrary, the reactionary and conservative newspapers revealed their opportunistic side as they colluded with those in power and subsequently was able to grow in number, which exacerbated the ideological antagonism in the peninsula.

Even in the immediate aftermath of April 19 Revolution in 1960, the reactionary and conservative newspapers had neither the will nor the capacity to assess and facilitate the varying opinions of the public. Instead, they filled their pages with phrases such as "denunciation of North Korea," "anti-Communism", etc., and avoided the issue of reunification.

Under these circumstances, the emergence of *Minjogilbo* was very timely. Covering various themes ranging from the reality of agrarian communities and North-South exchanges to reunification, the daily newspaper left a strong impact in the field of journalism at the time. Due to its refreshing coverage and editorial, in the month that *Minjogilbo* was founded—February 1962—more than 40,000 copies of the newspaper were published even without having previously secured a firm readership, and was on par with other major newspapers.

Minjogilbo was distinguished from the major conservative newspapers for its assessment of the U.S. presence in the Korean peninsula. It declared that the U.S. had backed Rhee Syngman in the South and had "contributed to the division of Korea", for which the U.S., along with the Soviet Union, bore the same political and ethical responsibilities. The economic assistance from the U.S., *Minjogilbo* argued, was out of their necessity and to their interest, and the true form of assistance must be oriented around consumer goods and policies that could help South Korean economy achieve self-reliance. When it came to the North-South problem, *Minjogilbo* emphasized two Koreas' ethnic and empathic bond and argued for active exchanges between the two, in opposition to the conservative newspapers that refused to tolerate Communism. *Minjogilbo* stressed that "the reunification was the task of our time," and proposed the reunification of the two Koreas into a non-aligned nation, which was based on their analysis of the rise of the Third World as a sign that the U.S. and the U.S.S.R. influence was being hampered.

Minjogilbo's activities were met with a positive response from the public, whose perception of the U.S. began to change. To the U.S., however, this was a problem, and the newspaper also had troubles with the Chang Myŏn regime, who remained suspicious of *Minjogilbo*'s seed funding. At one point, the publication of *Minjogilbo* came to a halt. Such circumstances exposed *Minjogilbo* as a primary target for Park Chung-hee, who seized power through a coup.

The day after the May 16 coup d'état in 1961, Park arrested Cho Yongsu, the chief executive of *Minjogilbo*, and took him to the "revolutionary court." On December 21st of the same year, Cho was executed without his family knowing. The verdict provided no evidence or motive of his purported crime and did not even follow the proper juridical procedures, making it an unlawful killing. Being aware of the U.S.'s suspicion toward Park Chung-hee's history of being a left-winger, he chose Cho Yongsu and *Minjogilbo* as sacrificial lambs to prove himself clean to the U.S. and to employ scare tactics before taking control of the press.

In November 2006, forty-five years after Cho's death, the Truth and Reconciliation Commission (Chinsil·hwahae wiwŏnhoe) decided that the revolutionary court's verdict on Cho after the May 16 coup was wrong, and the Korean court proclaimed that Cho was not guilty in January 2008. It took forty-seven years to have justice served.

Suppression of the Press and Rigging
of Public Opinion during
Park Chung-hee's Push to Amend
the Constitution

Once Park Chung-hee was elected president with control of the press by scare tactics and the use of violence, he rushed through the Press Ethics Committee Act (Ŏllon yulli wiwŏnhoe-bŏp) in 1964, which enabled the government to abort or stop publication of newspaper as they liked. Although the publishers resolved to resist the unjust legislation, Park successfully crushed their attempt. In August, 1964, reporters organized a coalition and declared, "in spite of the publishers' defeat, we will never surrender." Despite their resolution to resist the enforcement of the act, the press in the following decade fell subservient to the authority.

With the 1967 presidential election ahead, Park planned to prolong his rule and began ruthlessly suppressing the press. The chief executive of *Kyunghyang Shinmun* was arrested for violating anti-Communism laws, and the company was put on a public sale. Park's government also indicted Dong-A journalists who reported on the protests against the Japan-South Korea negotiation talks, assaulted the reporters, and even blew up one of the news company executives' house gate. Government agents came in and out of the editorial office and went through each and every article, column, etc.

The control of the press was effective. Park's victory in the presidential election of May 1967 was overwhelming, and the ruling Republican party secured enough seats to enable constitutional amendment in the June congressional election. The ground seemed fertile for the constitutional amendment, which would make possible for Park to serve three consecutive presidential terms.

With the press subservient to the regime, they no longer served as a watchdog and functioned instead as the government's public relations branch. With the state funding, *Chosun Ilbo* ventured into the hotel business, and *Kyunghyang Shinmun* became a pro-government newspaper once it was sold to a different group. In order to tame *Dong-A Ilbo*, Park arrested the editor-in-chief and sub-editor of *Shin Dong-A*, *Dong-A Ilbo*'s sister publication, for violating anti-Communism laws with their "Foreign Aid Corruption" and "China-U.S.S.R. Conflict" articles. Kim Sangman, the owner of *Dong-A Ilbo*, was forced to fire editor-in-chief Ch'ŏn Kwanu and other executive members who were thought to be responsible, and put up a statement of apology in regard to the *Shin Dong-A* articles.

In the aftermath of the constitutional amendment in 1969, the nation was in extreme chaos. Student protestors criticized the press for neglecting Park's constitutional violations. The press, in fact, actively supported and advertised Park's constitutional amendment. The ruling Republican party snuck into the National Assembly's 3rd annex at daybreak on October 21, 1969, and rushed through the constitutional amendment proposal.

Once Park Chung-hee seized control of almost all dailies, he also extended his grip on *Sasanggye*, a must-read monthly publication for all student protestors, whose extent of influence was on par with other dailies. To Park, *Sasanggye* was a big obstacle, as the writers of *Sasanggye* rejected the validity of the May 16 coup, criticized Japan-South Korea talks and deployment of troops to Vietnam. Park utilized a "refund tactic" whereby he mass-ordered the publication immediately after it came out and returned them three months later, which dealt a huge blow to *Sasanggye*'s finance. In May 1970, *Sasanggye* was shut down for publishing Kim Chiha's "Ojŏk" ("five bandits"), which was called out for violating the anti-Communism laws. The monthly publication that served as an outlet for anti-authoritarian democratic voice for seventeen years was no more.

Yushin Regime of Terror and Journalists' Desperate Resistance

In March 1971, university students began to protest for abolishing mandatory military training at school. Angered by the press's silence toward schools being garrisoned, the students performed *ŏllon hwahyŏngshik* ("execution of the press by burning") in front of the *Dong-A Ilbo* building in Gwanghwamun, claimed that the press had become "the regime's dog" and "authority's handmaiden," and declared them traitors to Korea and the Korean people. The young journalists who were holding off their anger from the *Shin Dong-A* incident and the constitutional amendment responded to the student protest by declaring the "protection of freedom of the press" (*ŏllonjayusuho*) and refusing government agents' entry to editorial office. This movement became nation-wide as journalists all over the country followed suit.

In spite of the young journalists' protest, Park dissolved the National Assembly, banned all political activities, and held a State Council meeting where he drafted and passed a new constitution—the so-called Yushin Constitution—in October 1972, in order to realize his dream of permanent rule. The new constitution gave Park the authority to appoint court justices and one third of the Members of the National Assembly, rights to dissolve the National Assembly under any circumstances, and power to rule by decree, effectively establishing the "imperial presidency."

In regard to the Yushin Constitution, the newspapers were filled with shameless pro-government slogans. On November 21, 1972, the Yushin Constitution referendum was held, where over 90% of the voters supported the new constitution, a result directly yielded by Park's tight control of the press.

The Korean Central Intelligence Agency personnels, counter-intelligence agents, security police, and detectives frequented news companies. Even reporting rights were denied to the press, which was instructed word by word to deliver the government statements and commentaries.

No state of emergency, however, stays forever. In autumn of 1973, student protests were organized into anti-authoritarian and anti-government movements. On October 2, five hundred students from the Seoul National University went on a protest where they criticized the dictatorship for threatening the people's right to life. Although one *Dong-A Ilbo* reporter reported on this event, the article was turned into a government statement titled "Arrest of Twenty-One Seoul National University Students." The

Dong-A journalists were furious, and resolved to track down every omission in a news article, immediately report on an arrest of any one of their fellow journalists, and stay put until their return. On the night of November 20, the Dong-A journalists drafted the second declaration of the "protection of freedom of the press", where they expressed their determination to refuse unjust government intervention and external pressure, and secure freedom of the press. When things didn't improve, they organized another meeting and drafted the third declaration of the protection of freedom of the press.

Other newspapers and broadcasting companies like *Hankook Ilbo*, CBS, and *Chosun Ilbo* responded to *Dong-A Ilbo*'s declarations. Religious leaders and other distinguished social figures launched a signature-seeking campaign titled "A Million for Constitutional Reforms" on December 24, for which they were arrested. Within the press, conflicts between the management and journalists intensified around the issue of whether an article or declaration would conflict with Park's presidential decree. When some journalists were unjustly fired or transferred to other posts due to the conflicts, they responded by organizing unions, which provided them with legal basis for their struggle. Although the newspaper managements and the Seoul City government collaborated to sabotage the unions at *Dong-A Ilbo* and *Hankook Ilbo*, which resulted in the loss of their legal status, they served as an impetus for organizing unions at media companies all over the nation after the June Uprising of 1987.

Dong-A Ilbo's "Declaration of Undertaking Freedom of the Press" on October 24, 1974 and Blank Ads

On October 24, 1974, the Dong-A journalists published "Declaration of Undertaking Freedom of the Press" (Chayuŏllon silch'ŏn sŏnŏn), in which they refused the state intervention, entry of government agents into their workplaces, and unlawful arrest of journalists. The declaration was a response to the arrest of Song Kŏnho, the editor-in-chief of *Dong-A Ilbo* who was responsible for reporting on the street demonstration by Seoul National University students. An excerpt is as follows:

"We declare that the unprecedented crisis our society today faces can only be overcome by freedom of the press...Fundamentally speaking, freedom of the press is not something that will be granted by the mass or allowed by the state, but a task that we, the press workers, must accomplish on our own. Therefore, we declare our resolution to not succumb to any form of pressure that seeks to set back the free press and to give all our effort to achieve the freedom of the press, which is one of the basic conditions of free and democratic society…"

As the declaration appeared on the cover page of *Dong-A Ilbo*, the movement spread to other newspapers, broadcast channels and media outlets. On the following day, the Journalists Association of Korea announced its support of the declaration, and announced four resolutions on a code of conduct for protecting freedom of the press, on urging the management for support, on organizing a task force, and on thorough reporting on violations of freedom of the press.

In November, priests, Catholics, students and youths from all over the country organized and participated in a mass rally called "Catholic Prayer Meeting for Human Rights Restoration". The Journalists Association of Korea's Dong-A branch insisted on reporting on this rally, and went as far as willing to risk a strike. Editor-in-chief Song Kŏnho accepted their demand and published an article reporting on the event in the society section of the newspaper. This was the moment in which Dong-A took the steps to break free from Park's control of the press.

The *Chosun Ilbo* journalists also started their fight. They erupted when the two journalists, Paek Kibŏm and Sin Hongbŏm, were fired in December for pointing out that the writing of Yushin Party's Chŏn Chaegu, which made an appearance on the previous issue of *Chosun Ilbo*, was a one-sided defense of the

Yushin regime. In response to their protest, Chosun fired additional sixteen journalists and suspended thirty-seven. The dismissed journalists announced a statement in March of the following year and declared that they would "fight to the last person, until the last moment."

Alarmed by the gravity of these movements initiated by *Dong-A Ilbo*'s "Declaration of Undertaking Freedom of the Press", Park Chung-hee began to strike back. In December 1974, *Dong-A Ilbo* and Dong-A Broadcasting Station faced mass cancellation of advertising contract from their sponsors. Shocked by the blank advertisement spaces on *Dong-A Ilbo*, readers expressed their support for Dong-A through fundraising and paying for subscription in advance.

In the following year, the so-called "encouragement ads" poured in during the new year. Religious organizations, political parties, social activist groups and even individuals offered sponsorship to put up their advertisement. A young girl visited Dong-A and offered her gold ring with a letter that said, "light shines the brightest in the dark." The help from the ordinary citizens ranging from bus attendants, students, restaurant workers to textile workers and tailors at the Pyeonghwa Market revealed how important freedom of the press was to ordinary people and also how big their desire for freedom of the press was.

What was happening to Dong-A was reported thoroughly by the foreign press like NHK, *The Times, Le Monde*, and *The Washington Post*, with details of the government's pressure on Dong-A's advertisement contractors, the journalists' struggles, and the "encouragement ads." In an interview with NHK, *Dong-A Ilbo*'s column editor Hong Sŭngmyŏn emphasized that the management's job was to protect their editorial, not the other way around.

However, the government refused to step back. Park pressed *Dong-A Ilbo*'s owner to have Hong replaced. When the cycle of protest, dismissal, and strike repeated, editor-in-chief Song Kŏnho resigned after proposing that the only way out of their current mess was to reinstate the dismissed journalists.

At daybreak on March 17, the sixth day of sit-in, a group of hired thugs stormed through the gate and forced journalists, producers and news anchors out of their workplace. Those who were forced out held a press meeting at the Journalists Association's office and announced a statement titled "Leaving *Dong-A Ilbo*, Overwhelmed by Violence". In the following afternoon, the dismissed Dong-A employees organized Dong-A Committee of Press Freedom Protection (Tonga chayuŏllon suhot'ujaeng wiwŏnhoe; Tonga t'uwi in short). The surviving members of the Dong-A Committee, which was initially made up of 113 journalists, continue their fight for their reinstatement and media freedom even to this date.

Seoul Spring of 1980:

Anti-Censorship Movement among Journalists

On October 26, 1979, Park Chung-hee was assassinated by Kim Chaegyu, the director of the KCIA. With the Yushin regime's end, South Korea was liberated from the dictatorship. Once the state of emergency was terminated, students and professors who had been expelled made it back to their campus. The politics slowly regained vibrance as the ban on political activities was also lifted.

As the first and foremost objective of democratization was coming to terms with the Yushin system, constitutional reform was the issue that attracted the most attention from society. This also applied to journalism. In January 1980, organizations such as the Korean Bar Association and Christian Academy drafted a proposal for constitutional reform that pivoted on the protection of editorial rights and the right to information and knowledge at the public hearing held by the National Assembly's Constitutional Reform Task Force (Kukhoe kaehŏnt'ŭgwi). The Journalists Association most actively publicized the issue of freedom of the press. With Kim T'aehong as the newly inaugurated chair, in April the Journalists Association hosted a lecture called "Constitutional Reforms and Freedom of the Press" where journalist Song Kŏnho claimed that the most important issue at that point was the freedom of the press, and professor Ri Yŏnghŭi emphasized the need for separation between the management and the editorial. Based on these lectures and the public hearing on constitutional reforms regarding the press policies, the Journalists Association drafted and submitted a proposal to the National Assembly's Constitutional Reform Task Force and the State Constitutional Reform Council (Chŏngbu kaehŏnsimŭiwi).

In spite of these nation-wide waves of democratization, the military, headed by Chun Doo-hwan, began to show their thirst for power. On May 16, the Journalists Association fiercely condemned the state censorship of media, and resolved to fight against censorship and eliminate the remnants of the Yushin system, stating that "realization of the press freedom is not possible without painstaking effort on our part." At this day's meeting where the Dong-A Committee and Chosun Committee journalists also participated, the Journalists Association decided to demand abolition of the censorship starting on May 20, and also to go on strike had their demands not met.

The day after their meeting, however, the new military government declared nation-wide martial law and arrested the Journalists Association executives. Nine of them were taken to a special interrogation facility in Namyeong district and severely tortured. Five of them, including chair Kim T'aehong, were sentenced to prison. Although the outraged journalists went on strike and announced a resolution of the press freedom starting two days after the May 18 Gwangju Uprising, they were either fired or transferred to different posts.

Whereas individual journalists resisted during the May 18 Gwangju Uprising, no media outlet ever resisted. What people had got instead were the pro-government outlets and military propaganda. The media, be it newspapers or broadcast channels, thoroughly misrepresented the Gwangju Uprising, describing the event as an insurgency and insulting the Gwangju citizens by calling them rioting outlaws. The misreporting continued throughout the Fifth Republic years, instilling the idea in the mind of Korean people that the Gwangju Uprising was an insurgency led by a group of outlaws. The local media in Gwangju remained powerless. After much struggle and out of despair, the journalists at *Chŏnnammaeil* (*Jeollanam-do Daily*) left the following resignation letter:

"We witnessed. With our own eyes, we clearly saw how people were dragged and killed like a dog. However, we weren't able to write a word on our daily. Out of shame, we give up on writing. May 20, 1980."

The Seoul Spring, which began with the assassination of

Park Chung-hee on October 26, thus ended. The ruthless and bloody massacre of Gwangju civilians extended to journalism, which forced the free press into hibernation. While dismissing by force journalists who were critical of the regime, Chun Doo-hwan induced voluntary submission from his press collaborators. Additionally, Chun sought to merge media outlets for an easier control, which resulted in dismissal of over 1,000 journalists from 39 press companies and shutting down of 172 publications across the nation. South Korea's press predicament seemed to have taken an irreversible turn.

Democratic Press Movement Association
and Exposing the "Reporting Guidelines"

The winds of change began to blow in the suffocating polit-ical and social climate of South Korea in 1983. With the prisons full of university students and Chun's political dissidents, South Korea's human rights issue was on the radar of the foreign press at the time. Being aware of such circumstances and Reagan's up-coming visit to South Korea in November, Chun Doo-hwan imple-mented a series of alleviatory measures, granting reinstatement, stays of execution and pardons for numerous political cases. Once freed, the pro-democracy figures organized the Democratic En-deavors Association (Minjuhwa ch'ujin hyŏbŭihoe) in 1984 in preparation for the upcoming congressional election.

The changing political and social climate exposed the re-ality of the corrupt links between the state and the media, which evoked the necessity of the press reforms for representing the people's voice truly. The journalists who were forcibly dismissed in 1980 initiated this movement, organizing the Association of the Dismissed Journalists of 1980 (80nyŏn haejigŏllonin hyŏbŭihoe) in March 1984 and demanding democracy, freedom of the press, and reinstatement of the dismissed journalists. Empowered by the movement, a group of progressive publishers along with the Association of the Dismissed Journalists of 1980, Dong-A Committee and Chosun Committee founded the Democratic Press Movement Association (Minjuŏllon undong hyŏbŭihoe; Ŏnhyŏp in short) on December 19, 1984, issuing a statement in which they claimed that "today's press has fallen subservient to those in power" and proposed the goals of founding alternative media, forming solidarity with the pro-democracy organizations, and facilitating the press reforms.

To escape the influence of the brainwashing media, workers, farmers and the urban poor began to publish their own newspapers where they expressed their own ideas and voices. Under these conditions, the Democratic Press Movement Association activists couldn't help but feel obligated to create an outlet that can represent the people, nation, and democracy against the dictatorship and the colluding media.

With their effort, the first issue of *Mal* ("words"), whose subtitle read "Stepping Stone of the Press for the People, Nation, and Democracy", came out in June 1985. While the founding issue of *Mal* took the Chun Doo-hwan regime by surprise, it provided courage and hope for the pro-democracy side and an opportunity for the colluding journalists to reflect upon themselves.

The founding issue enjoyed great success as it went in print again only a day after its distribution, successfully building reputation as a democratic media.

Mal was the only alternative publication at the time that was bold enough to cover topics that other mainstream media either tended to avoid or was unable to take on. One distinct example was its coverage of "the Reporting Guidelines" of the government. Around then, the Ministry of Culture and Communications' Public Relations Office (Munhwagongbobu Hongbojojŏngsil) issued reporting guidelines that specified not only what must be included—and excluded—in their coverage but also its form, content, and tone. The guidelines also stipulated minute details for any given news article such as its title, placement, inclusion of photographs, etc. For news broadcasting, the Ministry made them send to its office their queue sheet before the news went on air and assessed the size and arrangement of the visuals.

At one point, *Mal* had acquired copies of the reporting guidelines from Kim Chuŏn, a journalist from *Hankook Ilbo* who first discovered the files. Based on their acquisition, *Mal* published a feature article titled "The Reporting Guidelines: A Conspiracy between the State and the Media", which exposed all the reporting guidelines that were issued to each news company over the 10-month timespan beginning in October 1985.

Following the exposé, the *Mal* editorial office was seized, and *Mal*'s chief operating officer Kim T'aehong, executive committee member Sin Hongbŏm and *Hankook Ilbo* journalist Kim Chuŏn were arrested for defamation of the state and violation of the National Security Act. In response to these arrests, state-ments condemning the regime's oppression from the social ac-tivist groups and pro-democracy figures ensued. The foreign press also advocated for the three men's release. This occasion strengthened solidarity between the democratic movements and the free press activists. In contrast to the growing influence of the Democratic Press Movement Association and other alterna-tive media outlets, the distrusts of and disappointment toward the mainstream media deepened.

Launch of the Hankyoreh and Foundation
of the Korean Federation of Press Unions

In January 1987, Pak Chongch'ŏl, a Seoul National University student, died at the special interrogation facility in Namyeong district. When the police reported, "When we slammed the table, he went 'ugh', and died", people were outraged. Even the mainstream media that usually remained silent on issues like this covered the incident extensively. Kim Chungbae's column on *Dong-A Ilbo*, which begins with the plea, "Heaven and Earth, and people, please fix your gaze on his death", saw through the incident and sought to reach out to people who became increasingly desensitized by the regime's rule of terror and the daily use of violence. It was revealed that Pak was tortured, which resulted in the arrest of two police interrogators and resignation of the Minister of Home Affairs and the Director-General of the National Police.

However, the case was far from being closed. In May 1987, the Catholic Priests' Association for Justice exposed that there were, in fact, more police officers who participated in the torture—not just two, but five. When it was discovered that the police and the prosecutors tried to whitewash the case, people flooded the streets and shouted slogans like "bring down the dictatorship" ("tokchae t'ado") and "abolish the status quo" ("hohŏn ch'ŏlp'ye"). The street protests reached the peak when Yi Hanyŏl, a student at Yonsei University, fell after being struck by a tear gas canister on June 9. With the massive June Uprising on the 10th, the government surrendered on June 29, and gone with it were Chun Doo-hwan's attempts to preserve the status quo and prolong his rule.

The June Uprising was a wake-up call for the mainstream journalists and provided a fertile ground for the development of the labor movement in journalism. The media employees began organizing unions via legal means, starting with *Hankook Ilbo* on October 29, 1987, and *Dong-A Ilbo* on November 18, after which other newspaper and broadcast companies followed suit. In December 9, MBC employees founded a union for the first time at a broadcast company, followed by the KBS in May 1988. With their unions, the media employees undertook a wide range of activities to democratize the press, which, after a series of intense negotiations and struggles, culminated in the adoption of watchdog agencies and the measures to secure editorial rights.

During the course of negotiation and struggle, the media unions felt the need for solidarity apparatus that could undertake large-scale actions and had greater bargaining power, which led to the foundation of Korean Federation of Press Unions on November 26, 1988, with Kwon Young-ghil as chair, consisting of media unions from forty-one newspaper and broadcast companies. In the declaration speech given on its foundation day, the organization emphasized that "the press of this nation has walked the path of subservience and subordination ever since the 3rd Republic", and resolved to contribute to democratization by realizing freedom of the press. In November 2000, the unions under Korean Federation of Press Unions came to form the National Union of Mediaworkers, a large industrial union for media workers whose industries range from newspaper, broadcast and publishing to print.

Meanwhile, the broadcast unions in 1988 were actively demanding resignation of the parachuted chief executives. The union at MBC succeeded in driving out former government official Hwang Sŏnp'il and former Yushin party member Kim Yŏngsu, all of whom were parachuted into a chief executive position by the authority. As the broadcast employees strove to come to terms with their history of collusion with the Chun Doo-hwan regime, which earned them the humiliating nickname "state prostitute" (kwan'gi; 官妓), their effort into better program production culminated in MBC's *Mother's Song* (*Ŏmŏniŭi norae*) and KBS's *Gwangju Speaks* (*Kwangjunŭn marhanda*).

The foundation of Hankyoreh in May 1988 was another momentous event in the history of struggle for freedom of the press. The idea for founding Hankyoreh first came about when chair of Dong-A Committee An Chongp'il, detained in Seong-dong Detention Center at the time, was talking to his fellow media worker inmates in 1979. They came up with the specifics about the newspaper format, such as horizontal writing, hangul-only, synthetic editing, etc., in addition to the idea of adopting the so-called "people's share," a form of ownership that might be ideal for securing editorial rights. The 1985 article titled "Suggesting a New Media Outlet" in *Mal*'s founding issue encouraged An's idea by proposing a nation-wide movement for founding new media outlets, based on the supposition that "with the decline of mainstream media, the independent press through which workers, farmers, and people from other various fields express their voices is on the rise." The proposal materialized at the meetings among journalists and press representatives, which included Ŏnhyŏp chair Song Kŏnho, where they decided to adopt the people's share. The founding commission, consisting of fifty-six prominent figures from various fields, began seeking "ordinary citizen" investors, and the founding issue came out on May 15, 1988.

In a climate where the media was subservient to the state and the corporate power, *Hankyoreh*'s unprecedented form of ownership, people's share, resonated with readers. Their innovative format—hangul-only and horizontal writing—set *Hankyoreh* apart from the existing newspapers, leaving a huge impact in the field in general.

Struggles for Broadcasting Freedom
and the Foundation of Media Today

In January 1990, Roh Tae-woo's political party became a massive majority through the so-called "three-party coalition" (samdang yahap) and sought to take back control of the media. His first target was Sŏ Yŏnghun, the chief executive of KBS. Roh's regime dismissed Sŏ on the basis of absurd-sounding "irregular disbursement" to employees and appointed the former chief executive of *Seoul Sinmun* Sŏ Kiwŏn instead. After holding an emergency general meeting, the KBS union protested by forming a picket line and going on strike. Their attempt was met by the deployment of police force on April 12th and 30th. As the core union members got arrested, including the chair, the KBS union returned to production without success. Nevertheless, their month-long struggle in April dealt a serious blow to the Roh Tae-woo regime and served as a wake-up call for media workers for broadcasting independence from the state, precipitating the democratization of media.

The three-party coalition resulted in the social and political chaos as well. In April 1991, Myungji University student Kang Kyŏngtae fell after being struck by the police during the protest, causing a social uproar. Students and workers set themselves on fire in protest on a daily basis.

The emergence of three-party coalition also had changed the media landscape, as the managements began siding with the ruling party, leading to frequent conflicts between the management and the union. As a result, *Dong-A Ilbo* employees went on strike in January 1992, and Hankook Ilbo followed suit in February of the same year.

MBC was no exception, as the chief executive Ch'oe Ch'angbong exhibited a series of hostile behaviors toward the union such as violation of managing editor appointment policy and nonattendance at the Fair Broadcasting Commission meetings, which culminated in holding off the scheduled airing of *PD Note* (*P'idisuch'ŏp*) and firing the union's chair and executive secretary. Against such measures, the MBC union appointed an acting chair and went on indefinite strike on September 2, 1992, insisting on the reinstatement of the dismissed and abidance to the referral system for COO appointment. As many had expected, the strike went on for a long time. A month into the strike, the Roh Tae-woo regime deployed the police force of 1,600 to the MBC building, where they broke up the peaceful rally of union members on the first floor and arrested the leadership. Even after the arrest, the MBC union organized a special committee to continue their fight outside the company. After twenty days of struggle, the union dramatically reached a compromise with the management, and returned to work.

In the course of such struggles, the media workers were able to raise awareness for free and independent broadcasting and institutional measures to ensure fairness in broadcasting. However, the so-called "polinalists"—journalists whose political alignment was for the sake of their career advancement—voluntarily sided with those in power, while the media's increasing reliance on sponsorship foreshadowed the emergence of corporate power. As he was leaving *Dong-A Ilbo* in September 1991, Kim Chungbae warned that "the media now has to struggle against corporate power, a constraint that is far more fundamental than the political power against which it has fought up until this moment." The corporate power as a form of both ownership and sponsorship exerted strong influence on the media in terms of editorial lines, damaging the media's role as a political watchdog and social arbitrator. The conglomerate media represented by Chosun, JoongAng, and Dong-A legitimized those with illegitimate social privilege as "conservatives" and denigrated the progressives as "pro-North" (*chongbuk*) and "commies" (*ppalgaengi*), exacerbating the social unrest.

The media unions realized that the problem of corporate power, which sprung from the corrupt ties among the state, the corporate and the media as well as the disruption of the conglomerate media, would cause series harms to the formation of public opinion. Their realization led to the foundation of *Media Today*, which sought to inform the public with insights into the media climate and the media industry, including internal problems of media companies.

Media Today, whose founding issue came out on May 17, 1995, was assigned with the role of reporting on the state of today's media. In the foundation statement titled "Seeking Truth, Unconstrained by the State and Corporate Powers", the *Media Today* proclaimed, "Our target is the media's innermost structure, in which we will be able to reveal the true shape of power that animates the Korean press and the ways in which that power operates."

Decline of Public Broadcasting
and General Strikes of the Media Workers

In spite of the allegations of corruption, Lee Myung-bak rose to presidency in 2008, and replaced the chief executives of public broadcasting companies by force and through illegal means with his people.

When Ku Ponhong, who had led Lee's presidential campaign, was appointed as the chief executive of YTN in July 2008, the union strongly rebelled by picketing and going on strike. Ku Ponhong made a series of compromises such as agreeing to adopt the fairness in broadcasting policies and resuming *Clip Outbreak* (*Tolbaryŏngsang*), a short but popular satire program that had come to a halt due to the pressures from the government. However, the reconciliatory mood did not last long, as chief executive Ku, who was willing to reinstate the dismissed journalists and resolve conflicts with the union, suddenly re-

signed, only a year after his appointment. The sudden resignation was due to the regime's dissatisfaction with Ku, who was
unable to seize control of the organization. In contrast to Ku's
actions, Pae Sŏkkyu, the acting chief executive, was ruthless in
his suppression of the union. Pae removed the *Tolbaryŏngsang*
producer from his post and transferred news anchors to a non-
reporting department. Any program critical of the regime was
shut down, which sometimes was done by a phone call from the
National Intelligence Service.

KBS revived the program formats used to celebrate the president's accomplishments during the 5th Republic under preten-
tious titles like "The New Asia: The Era of Trans-Pacific Diplomacy"
(Sinasia, t'aep'yŏngyang oegyosidae) and "Internationalization of
Korean Nuclear Plants" (Han'guk'yŏng wŏnjŏn, segyero nagada).
They went as far as arguing for reinstatement of Rhee Syngman
as the nation's founding father and romanticizing Paek Sŏnyŏp, a
former imperial Japanese army officer, which were all part of the
conservative government's ideological agenda. The so-called
"presidential news" were always in the news headlines, whereas
any events or findings unfavorable to the regime were white-
washed.

Out of all media companies, MBC was the primary target
of government oppression. Faced with severe resistance from
the MBC union in the form of picketing and strike, the newly appointed chief executive of MBC, Kim Chaech'ŏl, swore to crush
the union, which meant, in his words, "modifying MBC's DNA."
Kim's intent corresponded with the regime's desire to turn MBC

permanently into the right-wing government's advertising tool, which was undertaken by illegal means such as departmental transfer and other unlawful disciplinary measures. Whoever was in his way was removed from production and reporting; any TV programs critical of the government were shut down; and the union was made incapable. The new employees had to pass the ideological litmus test.

Meanwhile, Lee Myung-bak sought to change the media landscape in order to prolong the conservative's seizure of power. His ruling party rushed through the media law revisions, which enabled the newspaper conglomerates such as Chosun, JoongAng, Dong-A, and Maeil to expand their business into broadcasting. Ch'oe Sijung, the chair of Korea Communications Commission, showered them with benefits such as "golden channel", "24-hour broadcast", "commercial breaks", and exemption from certain forms of broadcasting tax, which earned him the nickname "Prince of Communications".

Parachuted chief executives, intrusive interventions into broadcasting, union busting, and the media law revisions characterized the Lee Myung-bak regime's exhaustive control of the media, to which the media workers began resisting at last in 2012. The media workers at major broadcasting, communications and newspaper companies ubiquitously went on strike, which included KBS, MBC, YTN, Yonhap, *Kukmin Ilbo*, *Busan Ilbo*, etc. The workers resisted for the sake of the press freedom and independence, at their personal expense of wage and career advantages.

On January 30, 2012, the MBC union cut the starting line as they went on strike, demanding Kim Chaech'ŏl's resignation and guarantee of fair broadcasting. The strike went on for 170 days, breaking the record of the longest strike in the Korean media history. The people responded eagerly by participating in a signature campaign for Kim's resignation, which was able to collect over a million signatures. When *Infinite Challenge* (*Muhandojŏn*), one of the MBC's most popular TV programs, did not air for a long time due to the strike, people put up a banner in the street that read, "We Miss *Infinite Challenge.*" However, MBC's ratings fell significantly as the strike dragged on, which had made the union reconsider their plan as they cared for MBC's future. In July 2012, the union unconditionally put a halt to the strike and returned to work, where brutal acts of retaliation awaited.

The KBS union also went on strike, roughly a month after the MBC strike began, with the same demands. On the 52nd day of the strike, the representatives from four different Buddhist denominations sent their support and encouragement. On the 94th day, the KBS union returned to work and began resisting through their programs. Although the parachuted chief executive remained in place, the KBS workers were able to revive their investigative journalism team and shut-down programs, form the Fairness in Broadcasting Committee for Presidential Election (Taesŏn kongjŏngbangsong wiwŏnhoe), and abolish the regular radio speech given by the president.

The YTN union also organized a series of strikes for a total of fifty-five days over a period of six months, demanding Pae

Sŏkkyu's resignation. In March of the same year, the Yonhap union opposed chief executive Pak Chŏngch'an's reappointment. However, they decided to end the strike when the management agreed to adopt COO and editor-in-chief interim evaluation and fairness in reporting responsibility evaluation.

The returned workers, of course, were abused severely: according to the September 2012 statistics by the National Union of Mediaworkers, MBC dismissed eight and took disciplinary measures against two hundred and nineteen employees. KBS took disciplinary measures against one hundred thirty-three. *Kukmin Ilbo* fired three, in addition to about twenty against whom it took disciplinary action. YTN took disciplinary action against fifty-one employees, including the firing of six. The Yonhap News and *Busan Ilbo* took disciplinary action against thirteen and four, respectively. In that year's summer and fall, numerous journalists and producers left work, unable to return to work even after the impeachment of President Park Geun-hye in 2017.

The "Candlelight Revolution" and the Press

At a mass rally on November 14, 2015, people expressed their frustrations with Lee Myung-bak and Park Geun-hye, especially in regard to the controversial issues such as the Four Major Rivers Restoration Project, online opinion rigging by the National Intelligence Service, failure of the "energy diplomacy." the MERS outbreak, the Sewol Ferry Incident, the public school history textbook controversies, purchase of THAAD, the comfort women agreement, shutting down of the Kaesong Industrial Zone, the labor law revisions, busting of teachers' and public workers' unions, opening of the rice market, the dissolution of the Unified Progressive Party (T'onghap chinbodang), and the list could go on forever.

On this day's rally, some alleged that the Mir and K-Sports Foundations bribed the Park Geun-hye regime to adopt a series of labor law revisions that simplified redundancy procedures and enabled lower wages.

Eight months after the rally, several media outlets had discovered that not only these seemingly absurd allegations were actually true, but also the presence of Choi Soon-sil, President Park's personal friend, who was behind many of the decisions made by the regime, in addition to editing a substantial portion of the official speeches given by Park. On October 24, 2016, JTBC acquired and reported on Choi's tablet computer that contained not only Park's presidential speech files but also over two hundred government-classified files. What people had considered a mere conspiracy theory turned out to be true, and many realized that impeachment was inevitable.

On November 9, 2016, People's Action for Immediate Resignation of President Park Geun-hye was inaugurated, consisting of 2,382 organizations from all over the country. People lit over a million candles, shouting slogans like "Not Even a Proper Country" ("ige naranya") at Gwanghwamun Square. Park, however, was determined to stay, and announced that she would not resign by herself even if it meant she might be impeached. The rally grew twice in size to 2 million. It was too late when Park offered the option of "orderly resignation," as the angry crowd was unwilling to take it. On December 3, an unprecedented number of 2.32 million protestors held candles. The message was an immediate impeachment of President Park, which was met by the National Assembly's approval of impeachment on December 9, 2016.

Three months after the passage of the impeachment at the National Assembly, the Constitutional Court upheld the impeachment in a unanimous decision. However, the biggest contributors to this victory were neither the National Assembly nor the Constitutional Court, but were the few media outlets and the people who lit candles. JTBC, *Hankyoreh, and Kyunghyang Shinmun* did not fail to report on and confirm the lies and scandalous acts of Park Geun-hye and her associates, which provided strength and courage to the protestors. The alternative Internet news outlets such as Newstapa, Kukmin TV, *Ohmynews, Media Today*, and *Pressian* struggled against the news conglomerates and public broadcast channels that had fallen to pro-government sycophancy. With their help, the candles could grow from 100,000 to one million, and from one million to two million.

Even after the impeachment, the news conglomerates continued to spread fake news and propagate misreporting and false claims. Pro-Park advocate groups, or the so-called *t'aegŭkki* ("Korean flag") compatriots, began their activities as well. Faced with the presidential election, the news conglomerates revealed their true reactionary nature: while *Dong-A Ilbo* insisted on "investigation without detention" for Park, *Chosun Ilbo* preached about the necessity for respectful treatment of former president. The public broadcast channels such as KBS, MBC, YTN, and Yonhap News turned blind eye to the truth and framed the situation as the ideological face-off between the "candlelight" side and the "t'aegŭkki" side. The media landscape was far from what the candlelight protestors dreamed of, in which the nation's future seemed not so bright.

With Moon Jae-in elected as president on May 9, 2017, people began to organize movements to restore the public broadcasting. Over 240 civil society organizations, including the National Union of Mediaworker, Dong-A Committee, Korea Foundation for Press Freedom (Chayuŏllon silch'ŏnjaedan), Democratic Press and People's Coalition (Minjuŏllon siminyŏnhap), New Press Forum (Saeŏllon p'orŏm), Press Solidarity (Ŏllonyŏndae), and Media Consumer Rights Action (Ŏllonsobija chugwŏnhaengdong), joined forces to inaugurate People's Action for KBS and MBC Normalization. The apparatus organized various activities, including the weekly cultural event that began on July 21st, called out the public broadcast channels' board members who colluded with the Lee Myung-bak and Park Geun-hye regimes, and held them responsible for the sorry state of the Korean public broadcasting by submitting a petition to remove them to the Communications Commission.

As the public broadcasting workers went on strike again in 2017 and the civil society organizations brought pressure to bear upon them, the board members at the public broadcast channels who colluded with the past regimes began to resign. The newly formed Foundation of Broadcast Culture and KBS's board of directors adopted open and transparent procedures to appoint new chief executives. During the appointment process, no state intervention was made, as there was no room for such a thing.

Press Freedom Facilitates
All Types of Freedom

Looking back, all dictators had come to a tragic end. Rhee Syngman was exiled to a foreign country, where he spent the remainder of his life. Park Chung-hee was shot by his own subordinate. Chun Doo-hwan, Roh Tae-woo, Lee Myung-bak, and Park Geun-hye all served a prison sentence. The press freedom was the central theme throughout the nation's tragic history. All dictators sought to seize control of the press. There were opportunistic, colluding journalists and government officials with no virtue. Even the media outlets collaborated with corrupt leaders, with whom they cut ties and made new ones when needed. Such history repeated itself.

The reason why our media landscape became precarious and unstable was that no real attempt had been made to "purge" the media collaborators. Instead of being penalized for their history of collusion in the aftermath of Liberation, the pro-Japanese news conglomerates were able to expand thanks to the dictatorship. These news conglomerates collaborated with the dictatorship in suppression of democratic movements and fed on people's security fear. These conglomerates, whose ideological schemata involved denigration of their opponents as "commies," "pro-North" and "lefties", came to wield the power to establish and replace any regime as they desire.

One of the slogans at the candlelight rallies that brought down Park Geun-hye was the following: "The media too is complicit." In fact, rather than being accomplices, the news conglomerates were and had been the mastermind behind the long history of exploitation starting from the colonial era. Therefore, the first step into the reconciliatory effort must involve sorting out the opportunistic press collaborators and pro-Japanese news conglomerates.

In 2019, which marks the hundredth anniversary of the March 1st Movement, South Korea enjoys an unprecedented level of freedom of speech. With it, unfounded claims and fake news proliferate as well. Wild rumors now come under the guise of news-like visuals and formats, making it far more difficult to distinguish them from the truth. In today's media landscape, people make false claims as if they are true or make use of de-contextualized fragments of truth to suit their needs, driving our society into chaos and disruption.

The freedom of the press facilitates all types of freedom. However, the freedom to make false claims must not be allowed under freedom of speech. The role of today's media is to organize strategic movements that can filter out the distorted and fabricated from what Milton has termed the "marketplace of ideas".

Someone may ask, "Will the fight ever stop?" The history of humankind has not always been so pastoral. Throughout such history, struggles and organized movements have been everywhere, and will also be in the future, as long as there are those who dream of a better world. Their contributions move history forward.

References

Kim, Sae-Eun. "Journalism History: Korea." In *Media History and the Founda-tions of Media Studies*. Edited by John Nerone. Vol. 1 of *The International Encyclopedia of Media Studies*, First Edition. Edited by Angharad N. Val-divia. Blackwell Publishing, 2013.

———"A Reconstruction of Korean Journalism History through Dismissed Jour-nalists' Career and Life." *Ŏllon'gwa sahoe* 18, No. 4 (2010): 158–208.

Kim, Chongch'ŏl. *P'ongnyŏgŭi chayu* [*The Freedom of Violence*]. Ch'amŏllon Sisa–IN–puk, 2013.

Tonga chayuŏllon suhot'ujaeng wiwŏnhoe [Dong-A Committee of Press Free-dom Protection]. *Chayuŏllon* [*The Free Press*]. Haedamsol, 2013.

Minjuŏllon siminyŏnhap [Democratic Press and People's Coalition]. *Podojich'im 1986 kŭrigo 2016* [*Reporting Guidelines, 1986 and 2016*]. Tosŏch'ulp'an Ture, 2017.

Saeŏllon p'orŏm [The New Press Forum]. *Hyŏnjanggirok, pangsongnojo min-juhwaundong 20nyŏn* [*Field Archive, 20 Years of Democracy and Media Union Movement*]. K'ŏmyunik'eisyŏnbuksŭ, 2008.

—*Hyŏnjanggirok, sinmunnojo minjuhwaundong 20nyŏn* [*Field Archive, 20 Years of Democracy and Newspaper Union Movement*]. K'ŏmyunik'eisyŏn-buksŭ, 2009.

The May 18 Memorial Foundation. *5.18minjuhwa undonggwa ŏllont'ujaeng* [*The May 18 Democratic Uprising and the Struggle for Freedom of the Press*]. Tosŏch'ulp'an Simmian, 2014.

Wŏn, Hŭibok. *Choyongsuwa minjogilbo* [*Cho Yongsu and Minjogilbo*]. Tosŏch'ulp'an Saenuri, 2004.

저항의 한국 언론운동사

자유언론실천재단
언론운동사 소책자
제작팀

———

박래부
유숙열
이완기(대표 집필)
박강호
이명재

저항의 한국 언론운동사

초판 1쇄 발행 2019년 10월 10일

지은이   자유언론실천재단 언론운동사 소책자 제작팀
영역   장한길
발행   자유언론실천재단
주소   서울시 종로구 자하문로5길 37 (필운동 1층)
          전화 02-6101-1024 / 팩스 02-6101-1025
홈페이지 www.kopf.kr

제작 배급 (주)디자인커서
출판 등록 2008년 2월 18일 제300-2015-122호

ⓒ 재단법인 자유언론실천재단, 2019

ISBN 979-11-968105-0-4 03910
값 10,000원

이 도서의 국립중앙도서관 출판예정도서목록(CIP)은 서지정보유통지원시스템
홈페이지(http://seoji.nl.go.kr)와 국가자료종합목록 구축시스템(http://kolis-net.nl.go.kr)에서
이용하실 수 있습니다. (CIP제어번호 : CIP2019038279)

저항의

의

한국 언론 운동 사

자유언론실천재단

한국 언론사
: 치욕과 저항

한국의 언론 역사는 명예롭지도 자랑스럽지도 않다. 오히려 고통스런 치욕과 위선으로 얼룩져 있다. 오랜 세월 민주주의의 가장 가까운 벗이어야 할 언론이 비열한 독재정권과 결탁하여 민주주의를 배신하였기 때문이다.

독재와 타협한 언론은 광복 후에도 통일조국으로 가는 길을 방해했으며, 표현과 사상의 자유에 눈을 감았고, 많은 시민의 의로운 죽음과 인권 앞에 비겁하게 침묵했다.

굴욕적 과정에도 자유언론에 대한 신념과 사명감을 지닌 정직한 언론인의 끈질긴 저항이 있었다. 독재정권과 언론사에 의해 1천여 명의 언론인이 강제 해직 되어 거리를 떠돌거나 심지어 죽음을 맞는 쓰라린 고난과 희생 가운데도, 이들은 민주주의의 불씨를 소중히 간직해 왔고 오늘에 전해 주었다.

지금 민주 시민의 각성된 힘에 의해 독재 세력은 직접 마각을 드러내지 못하고 있으나, 자본의 지배력은 더 교묘하게 얽히고 광범하게 구조화하면서 언론자유를 조여오고 있다. 그러나 우리가 희망의 끈을 놓지 않는 것은 악조건에 대항할 우직한 언론인과 시민단체 간 유대의 힘도 커지고 있기 때문이다.

이 작은 책은 동시대인에게 한국 언론의 신산한 존재 방식을 알리고, 역사의 기록으로 남기면서, 민주주의에 대해 신념을 함께 하는 해외 단체들과의 연대를 위해 제작되었다. 자유

언론실천재단의 이부영 이사장이 제작을 제의하고 회원 박래부, 유숙열, 이완기(대표집필), 박강호, 이명재가 집필에 참여하였다.

만연한 허위의식과 역사적 위선에 맞설 공정한 언론 철학과 전통이 자리 잡기를 기대하며, 숙연한 마음으로 민주의 길에서 끝까지 부러진 창을 휘두른 선배 언론인들에게 경의를 바친다.

2019년 10월

집필진을 대표하여 박래부

서언

지배와 통제, 저항으로 점철된 언론 100년

사회를 감시하고 여론과 시대의 흐름을 전파하는 언론은 그 자체로 운동적 성격을 띠고 있다. 하지만 언론은 때때로 권력에 장악되거나 유착하거나 또는 스스로 권력이 되어 역사를 퇴행시키기도 했다. 그러기에 언론이 제대로 된 역할을 할 수 있도록 개선하고 바로잡는 '적극적 행위'로서의 언론운동은 어느 시대에나 있었다.

구한말, 언론의 역할은 사회계몽이었다. 정부 기관지와 민영신문들은 체제에 대한 인식의 차이는 있었지만 입을 모아 '자주독립'과 '개화자강'의 운동을 펼쳤다. 그러나 이러한 민족적 계몽언론들은 1910년 한일병탄을 전후하여 모두 퇴출되었다.

1919년 3.1운동은 한일병탄으로 인한 일제의 식민통치를 원천적으로 거부하고, 조선의 자주독립과 민주주의의 결의를 다진 역사적 전환점이었다. 대한독립을 외치는 시위가 수개월 동안 계속되었고, 수천 명이 시위현장과 감옥에서 목숨을 잃었으며, 조선독립신문과 같은 지하신문들이 곳곳에서 쏟아져 나와 독립의 의지와 당위성을 주창했다. 저항언론의 100년 역사는 이때부터 시작된 것이다.

3.1운동을 계기로 폭압통치에서 문화통치로 전환한 일제는 민족정기를 말살하고 한민족에 대한 정신적 지배를 강화했다. 그 시기 창간된 동아일보와 조선일보가 문화적 민족주의와 실력양성론을 내세웠지만, 기실 이것은 지주와 자본가들의 '기득권 보호'를 족쇄로, 한민족을 지배하기 위한 일제의 기만적인 통치전략이었다. 동아와 조선의 문화적 민족주의에 대해, 신채호는 '조선혁명선언'에서 "경제약탈의 제도 하에서 생존권이 박탈된 민족은 그 종족의 보존도 의문이거든 하물며 문화발전이 가능 하겠는가"라고 비판했고, 권업회보를 통해 의병과 민중의 투쟁을 전파했다.

일제와 미군정과 군사독재를 거치면서 꾸준히 항일운동과 통일운동을 펼쳤던 언론은 사회주의 계열의 진보신문들이었다. 그러나 이 신문들은 각 시기마다 정권의 표적이 되어 폐간되거나 경영난으로 자동 소멸되었다. 1927년 조선일보는

일제의 압력을 받고 반일 사회주의 언론인들을 무더기로 해고했다. 언론자유가 넘쳐났던 1945년 해방 공간에서도 사회주의 신문들은 반공을 한반도정책의 제일 목표로 내건 미군정에 의해 퇴출되었다. 4.19혁명 이듬해인 1961년 통일과 평화를 지향하며 혁신적인 활동을 펼쳤던 민족일보 역시 박정희 군사정권에 의해 빛을 보지 못하고 폐간되었다. 이러한 사회주의 신문의 퇴조는 지금까지도 보수족벌신문들이 신문시장을 과점한 채 극심한 냉전적 언론 풍토를 이어가고 있는 배경이기도 하다.

언론인들의 본격적인 조직적 저항운동은 그로부터 한참 뒤인 1974년, 동아일보와 조선일보의 언론인들이 박정희의 유신독재에 맞섰던 '자유언론실천선언'에서부터 시작되었다. 신문사에서 쫓겨난 동아와 조선의 언론인들은 동아자유언론수호투쟁위원회(동아투위)와 조선자유언론수호투쟁위원회(조선투위)를 각각 결성해 투쟁을 지속해 나갔다. 당시 해직된 113명의 동아투위 언론인들은 45년이 지난 지금까지도 자유언론을 위한 투쟁의 길을 걷고 있다.

1980년 12.12군사반란과 5.18 광주학살로 정권을 탈취한 전두환은 보도지침과 검열로 철저하게 언론을 통제했다. 그 과정에서 제작거부를 불사하며 저항했던 언론인들은 모두 쫓겨났다. 그러나 쫓겨난 언론인들은 '80년해직언론인협의회'

를 결성해 전두환 정권의 폭압적 언론 통제에 대한 투쟁을 이어갔다.

1970년대와 1980년대의 해직 언론인들은 언론운동의 밑거름이요 커다란 자산이었다. 이들은 언론자유를 짓밟은 독재와 맞서 싸우기 위해 의기투합했다. 동아·조선투위 언론인들, 80년 해직언론인들, 양심적인 출판인들은 1984년 민주언론운동협의회(언협)를 결성하고 더욱 정교한 조직적 투쟁을 전개했다. 언협은 기관지 〈말〉을 통해 전두환 독재의 폭력성을 세상에 알렸고, 보도지침을 폭로해 언론통제의 실상을 고발했다. 그 저항의 결실이 6월 민주항쟁과 함께 찾아온 1987년 체제다.

1987년 6월 항쟁 이후 한국사회는 형식적으로나마 독재와 군사쿠데타에서 벗어나 절차적 민주주의 체제로 접어들었다. 이를 기점으로 언론인에게 무시로 가해졌던 폭행, 강제구속, 고문 등 물리적 폭력은 사라졌다. 언론사를 활보하던 기관원도 자취를 감췄다. 6월 항쟁의 세례를 받은 제도권 내의 언론노동자들은 노동조합을 결성하여 '언론독립'과 '내적 자유'를 위한 투쟁을 활발히 전개했다. 이듬해인 1988년에는 국민주를 기반으로 한 한겨레신문이 창간되면서 진보언론의 기틀이 마련되기도 했다.

그러나 1990년, 3당의 야합으로 거대 보수여당이 탄생하

는 등 정치지형이 바뀌면서 역사를 거스르는 반동이 다시 고개를 들었다. 권부의 낙하산들이 방송을 장악했고, 경찰병력이 공영방송을 짓밟았다. 하지만 그 투쟁과정에서 더 단단해진 언론노동자들은 언론사 안에서 편집권 독립과 프로그램 투쟁을 치열하게 전개했다.

이즈음, 언론을 지배 통제하려는 또 하나의 세력인 자본권력의 문제가 대두되었다. 족벌 재벌 신문의 패악과 함께 정경유착과 경언유착(經言癒着)에서 힘을 키운 자본권력은 정치권력보다 더 원천적이고 영구적인 권력으로 변해갔으며 더욱 복잡하고 풀기 어려운 언론운동의 과제가 되었다.

1998년부터 시작된 김대중 노무현의 민주정부 10년은 나름 정권으로부터의 독립과 공정보도의 기틀이 마련된 시기였다. 자유를 찾은 언론은 왜곡된 근현대사를 바로잡았고, 독재시절 조작된 간첩 및 시국 사건들의 진실을 밝혀냈다. 매체들 간의 상호비평으로 언론사 간 침묵의 카르텔도 깨졌다. 그러나 이 시기에 보수족벌신문들은 더욱 수구화 되어 갔다. 이 신문사들의 노조마저 자사 이기주의에 포박돼 노조 설립 초기에 있었던 공정보도 활동은 점차 형해화(形骸化) 되어 갔다.

2008년 이명박 박근혜 수구정권이 들어서면서 더욱 구조화된 방식의 언론통제가 시작되었다. 신문시장을 과점한 권언유착의 보수족벌신문에는 방송채널의 특혜가 주어졌고, 공

영방송은 비판기능이 거세되어 다시 권부의 확성기로 전락했다. 보수일색의 이른바 '기울어진 운동장'이 만들어진 것이다. 이로써 언론의 공정성과 신뢰성은 수십 년 뒤로 후퇴했다. 부정, 부패, 거짓말, 무리한 정책 등으로 나라는 수구정권 9년 내내 시끄러웠다. 그 때마다 족벌신문과 방송은 정권비호에 앞장섰다. 이런 언론 현실은 '언론사 대파업'이라는 대대적 저항을 불렀고, 범국민적인 촛불시위로 발전하여 마침내 '대통령 탄핵'이라는 혁명적 국면을 맞게 되었다.

한국의 민주언론은 독재정권과 이에 결탁한 족벌언론사의 지배와 통제와 여론조작에 치열하게 저항했던 언론인들의 고난과 희생을 자양분 삼아 성장해 왔고, 지금도 이런 전통이 이어지고 있다.

언론계에 혁신을 일으킨
조용수와 민족일보

1919년의 3.1운동 정신은 이 땅의 언론인들의 의식 저변에 내재되어 있었다. 해방 이후에도 3.1정신으로 무장한 언론인들은 자주독립과 통일과 민주주의를 외치며 당대의 부당한 권력에 저항했다. 반면에 수구보수신문들은 권력에 순치된 기회주의의 모습을 보이며 양적으로 팽창하면서 이념적 편향성은 더욱 깊어갔다.

1960년대 4.19혁명 공간에서도 수구보수신문들은 다양하게 표출된 시민들의 주장과 요구를 담아내고 조율할 의지와 역량이 없었다. 보수신문들은 '통일'이라는 역사적 과제를 외면한 채 '북한에 대한 저주', '멸공' 등으로 지면을 채웠다.

이런 수구 일색의 고답적인 환경 속에서 민족일보의 등장

은 가뭄에 단비와 같은 것이었다. 민족일보는 농촌현실, 남북교류, 통일 등 다양한 의제로 언론계에 신선한 바람을 불러일으켰다. 민족일보가 1961년 2월 창간하자마자 구독자도 조직되지 않은 상태에서 4만부가 넘는 발행부수로 주류 신문과 어깨를 나란히 한 것은 이런 참신한 의제 설정과 논조에 기인한 것이다.

민족일보는 미국에 대한 인식에서 기존의 주류 보수신문과는 판이한 모습을 보였다. 민족일보는 이승만 단독정부를 세운 미국에 대해 '분단의 공범'이라며 "소련과 함께 정치 도의적 책임을 져야한다"고 주장했다. 미국의 경제원조도 미국의 필요와 이익에 바탕 한 것이라며, 소비재 중심의 경제원조를 지양하고 남한경제가 자립할 수 있도록 정책을 전환해야 한다고 비판했다. 남북문제에 대해서도, 공산주의와의 공존과 타협을 거부한 보수신문과 달리, 남북의 동질성과 정서적 유대를 강화하고 교류를 활성화해야 한다고 역설했다. 민족일보는 "통일은 시대적 과제"라고 강조하고, 제3세력의 부상으로 미·소의 영향력이 감소했다는 색다른 분석을 내놓으며 '중립화 통일론'을 대안으로 제시하기도 했다.

이러한 민족일보의 활약은 대중의 공감을 불러일으켰고 미국에 대한 인식을 변화시켰다. 그러나 미국에는 눈엣가시가 되었고, 민족일보의 창간자금을 의심한 장면정부와의 불화로

인쇄 중단 사태를 겪는 등 어려움에 봉착했다. 이러한 일련의 상황들은 이후 등장한 박정희 쿠데타 세력들의 먹잇감의 배경이 되었다.

1961년 5월 16일 쿠데타로 권력을 장악한 박정희는 쿠데타 바로 다음날 조용수 민족일보 사장을 연행하여 혁명재판부에 세우고 그해 12월 21일 가족들에게 알리지도 않은 채처형했다. 조용수에 대한 혁명재판부의 판결은 범죄의 동기도, 증거도, 절차적 정당성도 없는 살인행위였다. 미국을 의식한 쿠데타의 주역 박정희는 자신의 좌익 경력을 씻어내고 언론 장악에 필요한 공포 분위기 조성을 위해 조용수 사장과 민족일보를 희생양으로 만든 것이다.

조용수 사후 45년이 지난 2006년 11월, '진실·화해를 위한 과거사정리위원회'는 "혁명재판부 판단이 잘못됐다"고 결정했고, 2008년 1월 법원은 조용수에게 무죄를 선고했다. 무도한 권력에 의해 땅속에 묻혔던 정의는 47년 만에 되살아났다.

박정희 3선 개헌 때의
언론탄압과 여론조작

　폭력과 공포 분위기로 언론을 제압해 대통령 권좌에 오른 박정희는 1964년 신문발행의 정지 취소를 정부 입맛대로 할 수 있는 언론윤리위원회법을 날치기로 통과시켰다. 이에 발행인들이 중심이 되어 악법철폐투쟁을 결의했으나 박 정권의 각개격파로 힘없이 무릎을 꿇었다. 1964년 8월 언론사 기자들은 기자협회를 결성하고 "발행인은 항복했어도 우리 기자들은 항복할 수 없다"며 법의 시행에 끝까지 반대할 것을 결의했지만 이후 언론은 변함없이 권력에 순치된 길을 걸었다.

　1967년 총선을 앞두고 장기집권 구상에 몰두한 박정희는 반대 언론에 대한 무자비한 탄압에 나섰다. 박 정권은 정부

비판적인 경향신문을 반공법으로 걸어 사장을 구속한 뒤 공매 처분해버렸다. 이어서 한일회담 반대집회를 보도한 동아방송 관계자들을 기소하고, 취재기자를 폭행하는가 하면, 언론사 간부의 집 대문을 폭파하는 일까지 있었다. 기관원들의 편집국 출입이 일상화되었고 기관원들은 사설이나 기사 하나에도 일일이 개입했다.

언론탄압의 효과는 확연하게 나타났다. 박정희는 1967년 5월 대선에서 압도적으로 이겨 대통령 재임에 성공했고, 6월 총선에서도 공화당은 개헌 저지선을 뛰어넘는 승리를 거둠으로써 본격적인 3선 개헌작업에 나설 수 있게 됐다.

권언유착으로 언론은 비판기능이 거세되고 정권의 홍보도구로 전락했다. 조선일보는 정부차관을 받아 호텔사업에 나섰고, 경향신문은 경매 처분된 후 친정부 신문이 되었다. 박정권은 동아일보를 길들이기 위해 자매지 신동아의 1968년 '차관도입 비리' 기사와 '중·소 분쟁' 기사를 반공법 위반으로 걸어 편집장과 주간을 구속했다. 결국 동아일보 사주 김상만은 천관우 주필 등 관련 간부들을 해임하고 동아일보 1면에 신동아 기사에 대한 사과문을 게재했다.

1969년 정국은 삼선개헌으로 극도의 혼란에 빠졌다. 학생들은 박정희의 헌정유린을 언론이 외면하고 있다고 비판했다. 그러나 언론은 개헌 홍보와 지지에 여념이 없었다. 여당

인 공화당은 1969년 10월 21일 새벽, 국회 제3별관에 몰래 들어가 개헌안을 날치기로 통과시켰다.

일간지를 모두 무너뜨린 박 정권은 학생들의 필독서였고 일간지에 버금가는 영향력을 가진 월간지 〈사상계〉에도 손을 뻗쳤다. 5.16쿠데타를 부정하고 한일회담과 베트남 파병을 정면으로 비판했던 〈사상계〉는 박정희에게 눈엣가시였다. 박정희는 〈사상계〉가 출간되면 대량 주문을 했다가 3개월 뒤 되돌려 보내는 '반품공작'으로 〈사상계〉의 경영을 악화시키다가 1970년 5월호에 실린 김지하의 '五賊(오적)'을 반공법으로 걸어 〈사상계〉를 무너뜨렸다. 이로써 1950년대부터 반독재 민주화운동의 대변지 구실을 해온 〈사상계〉는 17년 만에 역사 속으로 사라졌다.

유신의 공포 속 언론인들의
처절한 저항

1971년 3월 대학가는 '교련철폐투쟁'에 휩싸였다. '학원 병영화'에 침묵하는 언론에 분노한 학생들은 광화문 동아일보 사옥 앞에서 "'권력의 주구', '금력의 시녀'가 되어버린 언론을 민족과 조국의 반역자로 규정하고 화형에 처한다"며 언론화형식을 가졌다. 신동아 사건과 3선 개헌파동으로 분노를 삭이고 있던 동아일보의 젊은 기자들은 이런 학생들의 외침에 '언론자유수호'를 선언하고 기관원 출입을 거부했고, 이 선언은 전국의 기자들로 확산되었다.

젊은 언론인들의 이러한 반발에도 아랑곳없이 영구집권을 꿈꾼 박정희는 1972년 10월 국회를 해산하고 정치활동을 금지시킨 뒤, 국무회의를 열어 유신헌법 안을 통과시켰다. 유신

헌법은 국회의원 삼분의 일 지명권, 국회 해산권, 법관 임명권, 무제한적 긴급조치권 등의 권한을 대통령에게 부여한 '대통령 1인 천하'의 법이었다.

유신헌법에 대해 신문지면은 낯 뜨거운 정부의 선전 표어들로 넘쳐났다. 그리고 그해 11월 21일 국민투표에서 유신헌법은 90퍼센트가 넘는 투표율과 찬성률로 통과되었다. 길들여진 언론의 효과가 여실히 나타난 것이다.

언론사에는 중앙정보부, 방첩대, 치안국, 정보계 형사 등이 자유자재로 들락거렸다. 보도 여부를 결정할 권리마저 박탈당한 언론은 계엄사령부나 정부의 발표문, 그들이 써준 해설 기사를 토씨 하나까지 보도해야 했다.

그러나 어떠한 긴장 상태도 무한정 지속될 수는 없는 일이다. 1973년 가을, 개학과 더불어 학생들의 시위는 반독재 반체제 움직임으로 격화되었다. 그런 가운데 10월 2일 서울 문리대 학생 500여명이 "국민대중의 생존권을 위협하는 참혹한 현실을 더 이상 좌시할 수 없다"며 유신독재를 비난하는 시위를 했다. 동아일보 기자가 이 시위 사건을 기사화했으나 기사는 엉뚱하게 '서울대생 21명 구속'이라는 정부의 발표문으로 둔갑하여 보도됐다. 분노한 기자들은 기사가 누락되면 누락 경위를 알아보고, 기자가 연행되면 연행 사실을 즉시 보도하고, 돌아올 때까지 기다린다고 결의했다. 11월 20일 밤에는

부당간섭 금지, 외부압력 배제, 언론자유 확보를 위해 모든 힘을 바치자는 언론자유수호 제2선언문을 채택했고, 그래도 상황이 개선되지 않자 다시 기자총회를 열어 제3선언문을 채택하기에 이르렀다.

　동아일보의 언론자유수호 선언은 한국일보, CBS, 조선일보 등 타 신문과 방송으로 확산됐다. 종교인과 재야인사들은 12월 24일 '개헌청원 100만인 서명운동'을 선언했다. 그러나 이들 종교인과 재야인사들은 긴급조치 위반으로 구속되었고, 언론사 내부에서는 기사나 성명서의 긴급조치 저촉 문제로 기자와 경영진의 갈등이 유발되었다. 갈등이 기자들의 부당전보와 해고로 이어지자 기자들은 합법적 투쟁이 보장된 노조를 설립하기에 이르렀다. 1974년 설립된 동아일보와 한국일보의 노조는 신문사와 서울시의 방해공작으로 법외노조가 되었지만, 십 수 년이 지난 1987년 6월 항쟁 이후 전국의 언론사에 노조가 설립되는 원동력이 되었다.

10.24 동아 자유언론실천선언과
백지광고

1974년 10월 24일 동아일보 기자들은 '자유언론실천선언'을 발표하고 '언론에 대한 간섭 배제', '기관원 출입 거부', '언론인 불법연행 거부' 등 3개 항을 결의했다. 이는 전날 서울농대 학생들의 가두시위를 동아일보가 보도하자 송건호 편집국장이 연행된 데 따른 것이었다.

"우리는 오늘날 우리사회가 처한 미증유의 난국을 극복할 수 있는 길이 언론의 자유로운 활동에 있음을 선언한다… 본질적으로 자유언론은 바로 우리 언론 종사자들 자신의 실천 과제일 뿐 당국에서 허용 받거나 국민대중이 찾아다 주어지는 것이 아니다. 따라서 우리는 자유언론에 역행하는 어떠한 압력에도 굴하지 않고

자유 민주사회의 존립의 기본요건인 자유언론 실천에 모든 노력을 다 할 것을 선언하며…"

선언문이 동아 1면에 기사화되자 이 운동은 삽시간에 전국의 신문, 방송, 통신으로 번졌다. 다음날 기자협회는 기자들의 자유언론실천운동을 지지한다는 성명을 발표하고, '언론자유수호를 위한 행동강령', '경영진들에 대한 촉구', '특별대책위원회 설치', '언론자유 침해 사건에 대한 빠짐없는 보도' 등 4개 결의사항을 발표했다.

11월에는 전국의 신도, 학생, 청년, 성직자들이 참가한 '가톨릭 인권회복기도회'의 대규모 집회가 열렸다. 기자협회 동아일보 분회는 제작거부까지 불사하며 이 기도회 기사를 중요하게 반영할 것을 요구했고, 송건호 편집국장은 약속대로 동아일보 사회면 중간머리에 이 기사를 올렸다. 동아는 마침내 유신독재의 입마개를 벗어던지고 자유언론으로 거듭난 것이다.

조선일보 기자들도 저항에 나섰다. 그해 12월 조선일보의 백기범과 신홍범 두 기자가 조선일보에 실린 전재구 유신정우회 의원 글이 유신체제를 일방으로 옹호하고 있음을 지적한 것 때문에 파면을 당하자 조선일보 기자들은 강하게 반발했다. 이에 조선일보는 다시 16명을 파면하고 37명에 대해 무

기정직을 내렸다. 쫓겨난 기자들은 이듬해 3월 성명을 내고 "최후의 1인까지 최후의 일각까지 투쟁하겠다"고 선언했다.

동아일보의 자유언론실천운동이 심상치 않게 전개되자 박정희 정권은 반격에 나섰다. 1974년 12월 동아일보와 동아방송에 무더기로 광고해약사태가 발생한 것이다. 동아일보가 빈 광고지면을 백면 그대로 인쇄해 발행하자, 시민들은 성금 기탁, 구독료 선납 등 다양한 방식으로 '동아 돕기 운동'을 펼쳤다.

이듬해인 1975년 새해에는 격려광고가 쇄도했다. 종교, 정당, 사회단체에 이어 시민 개개인의 1단 짜리 광고도 나왔다. 동아일보를 찾은 한 소녀는 끼고 있던 금반지를 빼놓으며 "빛은 어두울수록 빛난다"는 격려의 글을 남겼다. 시내버스 안내양, 학생, 밥집 아줌마, 평화시장 피복사 노동자 등 학생과 일반 시민들의 눈물겨운 격려광고는 그동안 시민대중이 언론자유를 얼마나 목말라 했으며 그 실천이 얼마나 중요한가를 깨우쳐 주었다.

해외 통신사들도 앞 다투어 동아사태를 전했다. NHK, 더타임스, 르몽드, 워싱턴포스트 등 해외 언론은 정부의 광고해약 압력, 언론의 투쟁, 격려 광고 상황을 상세히 보도했다. 홍승면 동아일보 논설주간은 NHK와의 인터뷰에서 "편집 방침을 지키기 위해 경영이 있는 것이지 경영을 지키기 위해 편

집방침이 흔들릴 수는 없다"고 강조했다.

그러나 정권은 물러서지 않았다. 박 정권은 동아일보의 사주를 압박해 홍승면 이사를 교체했다. 이후 기자들의 반발, 그에 따른 해고, 다시 기자들의 제작거부 등이 반복되자 송건호 편집국장은 "현 사태를 해결하는 길은 해임 사원들을 전원 복직 시키는 것"이라고 건의하고 사표를 던졌다.

동아일보 기자들의 농성 6일째인 3월 17일 새벽, 폭도들이 철문과 벽을 뜯고 들어와 농성중인 기자, 프로듀서, 아나운서들을 정문 밖으로 밀어냈다. 밀려난 동아일보 사원들은 신문회관 기자협회 사무실에서 내외신 기자회견을 갖고 '폭력에 밀려 동아일보를 떠나며'라는 성명을 발표하고, 이날 오후 동아자유언론수호투쟁위원회(동아투위)를 결성했다. 이후 동아투위 113명 중 생존해 있는 언론인들은 오늘까지도 자유언론 실천을 외치며 명예회복을 위해 투쟁을 계속하고 있다.

1980년 서울의 봄

언론인들의 검열 철폐투쟁

1979년 10월 26일 박정희가 김재규 중앙정보부장의 총탄에 살해되었다. 유신의 심장이 멈춘 대한민국은 해방의 땅이었다. 긴급조치가 해제되고, 제적 학생과 해직 교수가 학교로 돌아왔다. 정치활동 금지가 풀린 정계도 기지개를 켰다.

민주화의 제일 목표는 유신체제의 청산이었고, 각계의 관심은 헌법 개정에 쏠렸다. 언론계도 마찬가지였다. 1980년 1월 국회 개헌특위 공청회가 열리자 크리스천아카데미, 대한변호사협회 등이 '편집권 독립'과 '국민의 알권리' 등을 담은 개헌안을 마련했다. 가장 적극적으로 언론문제를 공론화한 것은 기자협회였다. 김태홍 협회장과 함께 새로 출범한 기자협회는 4월 '헌법개정과 언론 자유'라는 강연회를 개최했는

데 여기서 언론인 송건호는 "이 시점에 무엇보다도 중요한 것은 언론의 독립"이라고 역설했고, 리영희 교수는 "편집과 경영의 분리를 쟁취해야 한다"고 강조했다. 기자협회는 이날 강연과 4월 25일에 있었던 '언론조항에 관한 개헌 공청회'를 토대로 기자협회 시안을 마련하여 국회 개헌특위와 정부 개헌심의위에 제출했다.

이러한 전국적인 민주화 분위기 속에서도 전두환을 중심으로 한 신군부는 언론검열을 더 강화하면서 집권 야욕을 드러내고 있었다. 5월 16일 계엄 당국의 언론 검열을 거세게 성토한 기자협회는 "자유언론의 구현은 언론인 스스로 뼈를 깎는 노력 없이는 이루어질 수 없다"면서 검열 철폐와 유신잔재 일소를 위해 끝까지 투쟁할 것을 다짐했다. 동아 조선투위의 언론인들도 동참한 이날 회의에서 기자협회는 5월 20일부터 검열 거부에 돌입하고 관철되지 않으면 제작거부에 들어가기로 결의했다.

그러나 결의 바로 다음 날인 5월 17일 신군부는 비상계엄을 전국에 확대하고 기자협회 간부들을 검거했다. 기자협회 간부 9명은 강제 연행되어 남영동 대공분실에서 극심한 고문을 받았고, 김태홍 회장을 비롯한 5명은 실형을 선고받고 복역했다. 분노한 기자들은 5.18 민주항쟁 발발 이틀 뒤부터 제작거부, 자유언론 결의 등으로 저항했으나 저항한 기자들은

해고되거나 기자직을 박탈당했다.

5.18 광주항쟁에서 저항하는 언론인은 있었지만 저항하는 언론은 없었다. 한없이 비루한 계엄군의 홍보지, 신군부의 주구만이 남아 있었다. 언론은 방송, 신문 할 것 없이 5.18을 철저하게 왜곡했다. 광주항쟁을 '난동'으로, 광주시민을 폭도로 몰아 능욕했다. 이러한 왜곡보도는 5공화국 내내 지속됨으로써, 광주항쟁은 '불순세력에 의한 난동'으로 국민뇌리에 각인되었다. 광주의 지역언론도 무력한 것은 마찬가지였다. 저항 끝에 좌절한 전남매일 기자들은 처절한 심정으로 다음의 공동 사직서를 남겼다.

"우리는 보았다. 사람들이 개 끌리듯 끌려가 죽어가는 것을 두 눈으로 똑똑히 보았다. 그러나 신문에는 단 한 줄도 싣지 못했다. 이에 우리는 부끄러워 붓을 놓는다."

1980.5.20. 전남매일신문 기자 일동
전남매일신문 사장 귀하

10.26 사태와 함께 찾아온 '서울의 봄'은 이렇게 막을 내렸다. 이후 5.18광주민주화운동에 대한 무자비한 폭력 유혈 진압과 함께 자유언론은 오랜 동안 깊은 동면상태에 들어갔다. 광주를 폭력으로 제압한 전두환은 언론대학살을 단행했다.

전두환은 비판적 언론인은 강제로 해고하고 내부 협조자들은 자발적으로 복속하도록 유도하는 한편, 용이한 통제를 위해 언론사를 통폐합했다. 이로써 전국 39개 언론사에서 총 1,000여명의 언론인이 해직됐고 172종의 정기간행물이 폐간 조치 되었다. 한국 언론과 한국 사회는 치유하기 어려운 깊은 병 속에 빠져들었다.

언협의 활약과
보도지침 폭로

1983년, 질식할 듯한 정치 사회 환경에 변화의 바람이 불기 시작했다. 구치소와 교도소는 학생과 재야인사로 넘쳐나 나라 밖에서도 한국의 인권 상황을 주시했다. 이를 의식한 전두환은 레이건 미국대통령의 11월 방한을 앞두고 두 차례에 걸쳐 해금 조치를 단행했다. 각종 시국 사건에 대한 사면, 복권, 형 집행 정지 등의 조치가 이루어졌고 정치 활동 규제도 풀렸다. 억압에서 풀려난 재야는 1984년 민주화추진협의회를 발족하고 본격적인 총선 준비에 들어갔다.

이러한 정치사회 환경의 변화로 권력과 유착된 제도 언론의 폐해가 드러나면서 진정으로 민중을 대변하는 언론운동의 필요성이 대두되었다. 첫 움직임은 80년에 해직된 언론인

들이 중심이 되었다. 그들은 1984년 3월 '80년해직언론인협의회'를 창립하고 '민주화 실현', '언론자유 보장', '해직 언론인 원상회복' 등을 주장했다. 이에 힘입어 동아 조선투위, 80년해직언론인협의회, 진보적인 출판인들은 1984년 12월 19일 민주언론운동협의회(언협)를 창립하고 "오늘의 언론은 권력의 지배도구로 전락했다"면서 대안언론 창간, 민주운동세력과의 연대, 제도언론 개선 등의 목표를 제시했다.

사회 곳곳에서는 제도언론의 여론조작으로부터 벗어나기 위해 노동자, 농민, 도시빈민 등이 주체적으로 신문을 제작해 독자적인 자신들의 입장과 이념을 지면에 담았다. 이런 상황에서 독재권력과 제도언론에 맞서 민주와 민족과 민중을 대변할 언론을 만드는 것은 언협 활동가들에게 주어진 시대적 과제였다.

1985년 6월 언협의 노력으로 '민중·민족·민주언론의 디딤돌'이라는 부제를 단 〈말〉지 창간호가 세상에 나왔다. 〈말〉지 창간호는 전두환 군사독재정권을 놀라게 했고, 제도권 언론인들에게는 성찰의 계기를 만들었으며, 민주운동세력에게는 용기와 희망을 주었다. 〈말〉지 창간호는 서점 배포 하루 만에 재판(再版)에 들어가는 성공을 거두면서 민주언론으로서의 위상을 확고히 했다.

〈말〉지는 당시 제도 언론이 다루지 않거나 다룰 수 없는 중

요한 의제를 과감하게 보도한 유일한 대안 언론이었다. 그 중 하나가 보도지침 사건이다. 당시 문화공보부 홍보조정실은 전 분야에 걸쳐 특정 사건이나 상황에 대한 보도 여부는 물론, 보도의 방향, 내용, 형식까지 결정해 언론사에 지침을 하달했다. 지침은 기사의 선택, 제목, 내용, 위치, 분량, 사진 게재 여부 등 세부 사항까지 구체적으로 지적했다. 방송의 경우는 아예 9시 뉴스 큐시트를 정무수석실과 홍보조정실로 보내 뉴스의 크기와 배열을 심의 받았다.

한국일보 김주언 기자는 보도지침 사본을 묶은 서류철을 발견했다. 〈말〉지는 이 자료를 받아 '보도지침―권력과 언론의 음모'라는 제하의 특집 기사를 통해 1985년 10월부터 10개월간 각 언론사에 시달된 보도지침을 폭로했다.

이 폭로로 〈말〉지 편집실은 압수수색을 당했고, 김태홍 사무국장과 신홍범 실행위원, 김주언 기자는 국가보안법 위반 및 국가모독죄로 구속되었다. 이러한 정권의 탄압에 시민사회 및 재야는 잇따라 성명을 발표했다. 나라 밖에서도 세 언론인의 석방을 촉구했다. 이 사건을 계기로 언론운동진영과 민주화세력 간의 연대는 더욱 공고해졌다. 언협을 비롯한 재야언론인들의 신뢰와 영향력은 더욱 높아진 반면 제도언론에 대한 사회적 불신과 불만은 더욱 고조되었다.

한겨레신문 창간과
언노련의 창립

1987년 1월, 남영동 대공분실에서 서울대학교 학생 박종철이 사망했다. "책상을 탁 치니 억하고 죽었다"는 경찰의 발표에 시민들은 분노했다. 검열과 보도지침으로 침묵하고 있던 제도 언론도 이 사건을 크게 다루었다. "하늘이여 땅이여 사람들이여 저 죽음을 응시해 주기 바란다"로 시작하는 김중배 동아일보 논설위원의 칼럼은 박종철 사망 사건의 본질을 꿰뚫었고, 폭압적 공포정치에 숨죽이고 일상화된 국가폭력에 무감각해진 시민들의 양심을 깨웠다. 고문 사실이 드러났고, 수사 경관 2명이 구속되었으며, 치안본부장과 내무부장관은 해임됐다.

그러나 그것이 끝이 아니었다. 1987년 5월, 천주교 정의구

현사제단이 고문 가담 경관이 2명이 아니라 5명이었다는 사실을 새롭게 폭로한 것이다. 경찰과 검찰의 축소 은폐 사실이 드러나자 거리로 쏟아져 나온 시민들은 '독재타도'와 '호헌철폐'를 외쳤다. 시위는 6월 9일 이한열 연세대학교 학생이 경찰의 최루탄에 쓰러진 다음 날 정점에 달했다. 6.10항쟁은 마침내 철옹성 같았던 정권으로부터 6월 29일 항복선언을 받았고, 전두환의 호헌과 신군부의 장기집권 기도는 좌절되었다.

6.10항쟁은 제도권 언론인들의 각성과 언론노동운동을 싹틔우는 계기가 되었다. 언론사 구성원들은 언론운동을 위한 합법적 수단으로 노조를 결성했다. 1987년 10월 29일 한국일보를 필두로 11월 18일에는 동아일보에 노조가 설립되었고 타 신문과 방송으로 확산되었다. 12월 9일에는 MBC가 방송사 최초로 노조를 설립했고 1988년 5월에는 KBS에 노조가 설립됐다. 언론노동자들은 노조를 중심으로 언론민주화를 위한 다양한 활동을 펼쳤고, 불공정 보도에 대한 감시기구, 편집권독립을 위한 견제장치를 만들었다. 이를 일구어내는 데는 치열한 협상과 투쟁이 병행되었다.

투쟁 과정에서 더 높은 수준의 협상력과 더 큰 규모의 단결을 위한 연대기구의 필요를 느낀 언론사 노조들은 1988년 11월 26일 전국언론노동조합연맹(언노련)을 결성하고 권영길 준비위원장을 초대 위원장으로 선출했다. 전국의 41개 신문

사와 방송사 노동조합들로 결성된 언노련은 창립 선언문에서 "이 땅의 언론은 3공화국 이래 이십 수 년 간 예속과 굴종의 길을 걸어왔다"고 강조하면서 언론자유 실천을 통해 사회 민주화에 이바지할 것을 다짐했다. 이후 언노련 산하 노조들은 2000년 11월 신문, 방송, 출판, 인쇄까지를 아우르는 전국언론노조를 결성해 언론 관련 거대 단일산별노조를 조직하기에 이른다.

한편, 1988년 방송노조는 낙하산 사장 퇴진투쟁을 활발하게 전개했다. MBC노조는 청와대 출신 황선필과 유신정우회 출신 김영수 등 낙하산 사장들을 연달아 쫓아냈다. '정권의 관기(官妓)'라는 치욕스런 별칭을 달고 있었던 방송노동자들은 독재정권 시절 자신들이 저질렀던 과오를 반성하며 프로그램 투쟁에도 힘을 쏟았다. MBC의 〈어머니의 노래〉와 KBS의 〈광주는 말한다〉는 바로 그 투쟁의 산물이었다.

1988년 5월 한겨레신문 창간은 언론운동사의 또 하나의 획기적 사건이었다. 한겨레신문의 최초 구상은 1979년 서울 성동구치소에 수감 중이었던 안종필 동아투위 위원장이 함께 구속된 언론 동지들과 옥중 대화를 나누는 과정에서 처음 나왔다. 여기서 가로쓰기, 한글 전용, 종합 편집, 출입처 제도 폐지 등 구체적인 신문 제작 방식이 언급됐고, 국민 다수의 출자로 편집권 독립을 이룰 수 있는 소유구조에 대한 의견도

나왔다. 한겨레신문 창간을 공론화하는 데는 〈말〉지 창간호의 역할이 컸다. 1985년 〈말〉지 창간호는 '새 언론기관의 창설을 제안한다'에서 "제도 언론의 외면으로 노동자 농민 등 여러 분야에서 자신들의 목소리를 전하는 자생적인 언론이 활발히 전개되고 있다"고 전제하고, 새로운 언론기관을 만들기 위한 '범민중운동'을 제안했다. 이 제안은 송건호 언협 의장과 몇몇 단체 대표 및 언론인들 모임에서 구체화되었고, 196명으로 '창간발의준비위원회'가 구성되어 국민주 공모를 결의했다. 이후 각계 대표 56명으로 구성된 '창간위원회'는 본격적인 주식 모집에 나섰고 1988년 5월 15일 창간호를 내게 됐다.

정권과 자본에 종속된 언론환경 속에서 국민주라는 세계 유례없는 소유구조를 가진 한겨레신문은 민주, 민족, 민중의 노선을 지향하면서 독자들에게 커다란 반향을 불러일으켰고, 한글전용, 가로쓰기 등 기존 제도권 신문과의 차별화로 신문업계에도 큰 변화를 일으켰다.

방송독립 투쟁과
미디어오늘 창간

1990년 1월, 인위적인 3당 합당으로 거대 여당이 된 노태우는 권부의 지배력을 되찾기 위한 수단으로 방송을 지목했다. 그 첫 번째 표적이 구성원들로부터 좋은 평가를 받고 있던 KBS 서영훈 사장이었다. 노 정권은 직원 법정수당을 '변칙지급'했다는 터무니없는 이유를 들어 서영훈 사장을 해임하고 후임으로 서울신문 사장으로 있던 서기원을 임명했다. 이에 KBS노조는 비상 총회를 열고 낙하산 사장 서기원의 출근 저지, 제작 거부 등의 투쟁을 전개했다. 그러나 4월 12일과 30일 연이어 경찰 병력이 투입되었다. 게다가 노조위원장을 비롯한 노조 간부들의 구속으로 투쟁 동력을 잃은 KBS노조는 결국 '낙하산 사장 퇴진'이라는 가시적 성과를 거두지

못한 채 제작에 복귀하고 말았다. 그렇지만 KBS 4월 투쟁은 공권력에 맞선 한 달 남짓한 투쟁으로 노태우 정권의 도덕성에 치명적인 타격을 주었다. 구성원들은 방송독립의 필요성을 절감하게 되었으며 이는 향후 방송민주화의 자양분이 되었다.

3당 야합은 정치사회적으로도 수많은 갈등과 혼란을 야기했다. 1991년 4월 명지대생 강경대가 시위 도중 경찰의 쇠파이프에 맞아 숨지는 사건이 발생하면서 시국은 한 치를 내다볼 수 없는 상황이 되었다. 이로 인해 학생과 노동자들이 하루가 멀다 하고 분신하여 목숨을 잃는 분신정국이 이어졌다.

거대 여당의 출현으로 정치 균형이 깨지자 언론사 경영진의 태도도 달라지면서 노사갈등이 잦아졌다. 1992년 1월 동아일보에서, 2월 한국일보에서 연이어 파업사태가 벌어지게 된 것은 이런 경영진의 태도 변화가 주요한 원인으로 작용했다.

MBC도 예외는 아니었다. MBC 최창봉 사장은 국장추천제 위반, 공방협 불참 등 노조를 무시하는 태도를 보이더니 급기야 방송 시간까지 예고된 〈피디수첩〉의 방송 보류를 지시해 노조와 갈등을 유발하고, 노조 사무국장과 위원장을 차례로 해고했다. 이에 MBC노조는 위원장 직무대행체제로 전환한 후, 1992년 9월 2일 해고자 복직과 국장추천제의 관철을 걸

고 무기한 전면파업에 돌입했다. 예측대로 파업은 장기화됐고 파업 한 달째 되는 10월 2일, 노태우정권은 1,600여명의 경찰을 투입해 MBC 1층 민주의 터에서 평화적인 집회를 하고 있던 조합원들을 강제 해산시키고 파업지도부를 구속했다. 그러나 MBC노조는 파업지도부가 구속된 후에도 비상대책위원회를 꾸려 치열한 장외투쟁을 벌였다. MBC노조는 그렇게 20일을 더 싸운 끝에 회사와 대타협을 이루고 현장에 복귀했다.

이러한 투쟁 과정에서 언론사 구성원들의 언론의 자유와 독립에 대한 인식은 크게 증진되었다. 공정보도를 담보할 제도적 장치도 만들어졌다. 그러나 개인의 영달을 꿈꾸는 일부 '폴리널리스트'(Polinalist)들은 자발적으로 권력과 유착했고, 언론의 광고 의존도가 높아지면서 경언유착(經言癒着)도 심화됐다. 이러한 언론 현실은 언론을 지배 통제하려는 또 하나의 세력인 자본권력의 등장을 의미하고 있었다. 이에 대해 김중배 동아일보 편집국장은 1991년 9월 동아일보를 떠나면서 "언론은 이제 권력과의 싸움에서 보다 원천적 제약 세력인 자본과의 힘겨운 싸움을 벌이지 않으면 안 되는 시기에 접어들었다"고 선언했다. 사주와 광고주로 언론의 경제적 생명줄을 쥔 자본권력은 언론의 편집방향을 좌지우지하면서 언론의 권력에 대한 감시 비판 기능을 무력화하고 사회적 통합 조율 기

능을 마비시켰다. 특히 조중동으로 대변되는 족벌언론은 사회 상층부의 '부당한 기득권'을 '보수'로 정당화하고 '진보'를 '종북 빨갱이'로 매도하면서 사회 분열을 증폭시켰다.

언론사 노조들은 이러한 권언유착(勸言癒着)과 경언유착(經言癒着)에 따른 자본권력의 문제, 그리고 족벌언론의 분열적 메시지들이 사회적 여론 형성에 심각한 악영향을 미칠 것이라는데 공감하고, 기사와 논평, 언론사 내부의 병폐, 언론환경, 언론산업에 이르기까지, 언론심층의 문제들을 대중에게 알릴 전문매체 〈미디어오늘〉을 창간하기로 결의했다.

〈미디어오늘〉은 언론비평 전문 매체로서 언론의 실상을 일반에게 전파하는 역할을 부여받았고 1995년 5월 17일 창간호가 세상에 나왔다. 〈미디어오늘〉은 '권력, 자본을 뛰어넘어 진실 되게'라는 제하의 창간사에서 "우리가 오늘부터 향하고자 하는 곳은 언론의 '심층'이다. 그곳에서 우리는 한국의 언론을 작동시키는 본질적인 힘의 실체와 그것들의 운동방식을 밝혀내고자 한다"고 선언했다.

공영방송의 쇠락,
언론사 대파업

2008년 숱한 비리 의혹에도 불구하고 집권한 이명박은 불법과 강권을 동원해 임기가 남은 공영방송사 사장들을 해임하고 그 자리에 낙하산 사장들을 앉혔다.

2008년 7월 이명박 대선캠프 출신 구본홍이 YTN사장으로 선임되자 노조는 출근 저지와 제작 거부로 거세게 반발했다. 이에 구본홍은 노조와 '공정방송을 위한 노사 협약'을 체결하고 중지했던 〈돌발영상〉을 재개하는 등 타협책으로 노조와의 갈등을 풀었다. 그러나 이런 화합의 분위기는 오래 가지 못했다. 해고자를 복직시키고 노사갈등을 마무리하려던 구 사장이 취임 1년 만에 돌연 사퇴한 것이다. YTN을 장악하지 못한 구 사장의 행보에 정권의 비위가 틀어진 것이 사퇴의 근본 원

인이었다. 이후 사장 직무대행을 맡은 배석규 전무는 철저하게 노조를 탄압했다. 배 전무는 〈돌발영상〉 피디를 대기 발령하고, 앵커는 비보도 부서로 쫓아냈다. 정권 비판적 프로그램은 폐지됐고, 국정원 전화 한 통으로 방송중단 지시가 내려지기도 했다.

KBS에서는 대통령 치적을 홍보하기 위해 5공 시절 보도 특집 형태의 프로그램이 재현되었다. '신아시아, 태평양 외교시대', '한국형 원전, 세계로 나가다' 등 알맹이 없는 보도 특집이 제작 방송됐다. 또한 이승만 복권, 이승만 국부론, 심지어는 친일파 백선엽을 미화하는 프로그램이 보수정권의 이념 홍보 수단으로 이용되었다. 사장의 편집 개입은 5공 시절의 보도지침을 방불케 했다. 대통령 뉴스는 전진배치, 정권에 불리한 기사는 축소 또는 보도 불가 등의 지침이 일상적으로 이루어졌다.

가장 극심한 탄압이 자행된 곳은 MBC였다. 2010년 2월 선임된 김재철 MBC사장은 출근저지, 파업 등 노조의 격렬한 저항을 받은 뒤 "MBC의 유전자를 바꾸겠다"며 노조 파괴를 기도했다. 이는 MBC를 우파정권의 항구적 홍보 도구로 만들고자 하는 정권의 욕구이기도 했다. 이를 위해 불법징계, 부당전보 등의 불법행위가 저질러졌다. 김 사장의 뜻에 걸림돌이 되는 사람은 취재 제작 현장에서 배제되었고, 정권 비판

프로그램은 폐지되었으며, 노조는 무력화되었다. 사원 채용 과정에서도 사상과 지역에 대한 철저한 검증이 이루어졌다.

한편, 이명박 정권은 보수우파의 영구집권을 위해 미디어 환경을 보수일색으로 재편하는 작업에 나섰다. 이를 위해 신문 방송 겸영을 허용한 미디어법을 날치기로 통과시켰고, 조선, 중앙, 동아, 매일경제 등 4개 보수신문들에 종합편성채널(종편)을 안겨주었다. '방통대군'이라는 별칭의 최시중 방송통신위원회 위원장은 종편에 '황금채널', '24시간 종일방송', '중간광고', '방송발전기금 면제' 등 온갖 특혜를 부여해 보수성향의 친정부 방송을 강화시킴으로써 우파정권의 장기집권 발판을 만들었다.

낙하산 사장, 방송의 무단개입, 노조말살, 미디어법 날치기 등 이명박 정권의 전방위적 언론장악 기도에 언론사 구성원들은 2012년 마침내 저항을 시작했다. KBS, MBC, YTN, 연합뉴스, 국민일보, 부산일보 등 주요 방송 통신 신문사들이 동시다발적으로 파업에 돌입했다. 언론사 노동자들은 언론의 자유와 독립을 위해 무임금과 인사 불이익 등 개인의 손해를 감수하면서 기꺼이 파업에 동참했다.

2012년 1월 30일, MBC노조가 김재철 사장 퇴진과 공정방송을 내걸고 앞장서 파업에 돌입했다. 이 파업은 170일까지 지속되면서 방송사상 최장기 파업으로 기록되었다. 시민의

호응도 컸다. 김재철 퇴진 서명은 100만 명이 넘었고 자발적인 후원금도 쏟아졌다. MBC 인기프로그램인 '무한도전'의 불방이 계속되자 길거리에는 "보고 싶다 무한도전"이라는 현수막이 걸리기도 했다. 그러나 파업이 장기화되면서 MBC의 시청률은 끝없이 추락했다. MBC의 미래를 고려하지 않을 수 없었던 노조는 싸움의 지속 여부를 심각하게 고민한 끝에 2012년 7월 아무런 조건 없이 파업을 중단했다. 그러나 복귀한 조합원들에게는 잔인한 보복이 기다리고 있었다.

MBC 파업 돌입 한 달여 뒤, KBS도 낙하산 사장 퇴진을 요구하며 총파업에 돌입했다. 파업 52일차에는 불교 4대 종단의 대표들이 나와 지지와 성원을 보냈다. KBS노조는 94일 만에 파업을 종료하고 프로그램 투쟁으로 전환했다. KBS노조는 낙하산 사장 퇴진에 실패했지만 대선공정방송위원회 구성, 탐사보도팀 및 폐지 프로그램 부활, 대통령 주례 라디오 연설 폐지 등에 합의하는 성과를 거뒀다.

YTN노조도 배석규 퇴진을 내걸고 6개월 동안 10여 차례에 걸쳐 55일 파업을 벌이며 싸웠다. 같은 해 3월 박정찬 사장 연임을 반대한 연합뉴스 노조는 '편집총국장 중간평가제'와 '공정보도 책임평가제'를 실시하기로 합의하고 파업 100일 만에 업무에 복귀했다.

저항한 구성원들은 극심한 박해를 받았다. 언론노조 집계

에 따르면, 2012년 9월 기준으로 MBC는 8명 해고에 219명을 징계했다. KBS도 징계자가 133명에 이르렀다. 국민일보는 해고 3명을 포함해 20여명을 징계했고 YTN은 해고 6명 등 51명을 징계했다. 연합뉴스는 13명을 징계했고 부산일보에서도 편집국장을 대기발령하는 등 4명을 징계했다. 그해 여름과 가을, 수많은 기자와 피디들이 현장을 떠났고, 박근혜 대통령이 파면당한 후인 2017년까지도 쫓겨난 언론인들은 복귀하지 못했다.

촛불혁명과
언론의 활약

2015년 11월 14일 열린 민중총궐기대회에서 시민들은 이명박 박근혜 정권 기간 쌓인 불만을 한꺼번에 토해냈다. 4대강 개발, 자원외교의 혈세낭비, 국정원댓글, 세월호 참사, 메르스 사태, 사드, 위안부 야합, 개성공단 폐쇄, 역사교과서 국정화, 노동개악, 전교조·공무원노조 탄압, 쌀 개방, 통합진보당 해산 등 이날 쏟아져 나온 시민들의 불만은 헤아릴 수 없을 정도였다.

특히 이날 궐기대회에서는 박근혜 정권이 '정리해고 확대', '낮은 임금' 등 노동개악 정책을 서두른 배경으로, 재벌로부터 미르·K스포츠재단 설립을 위해 뇌물을 받고 그 대가로 재벌의 민원을 해결해 준 것이라는 의혹이 주목을 끌었다.

이로부터 8개월이 지난 2016년 7월부터 이 의혹은 몇몇 언론의 보도에 의해 사실로 드러났다. 뿐만 아니라 그 과정에서 사인인 최순실이 대통령의 연설문을 사전에 열람하고, 그 중 상당 부분을 수정했으며, 정부의 주요 인사와 정책에도 깊숙이 개입했다는 사실이 드러났다. 2016년 10월 24일 JTBC가 확보해 보도한 최순실의 태블릿PC에는 드레스덴 연설문을 포함해 44개의 대통령연설문 파일과 국가의 극비 문서파일 200여개가 들어 있었다. 촛불시민들은 그동안 의혹으로만 여겼던 대통령의 국정농단이 모두 사실이었고 박 대통령에 대한 탄핵이 불가피해졌음을 확인했다.

2016년 11월 9일 전국의 2,382개 단체로 구성된 퇴진행동(박근혜정권퇴진 비상국민행동)이 발족했다. 광화문광장에는 100만이 넘는 촛불이 타올랐다. 시민들은 "이게 나라냐"고 외쳤다. 그러나 청와대는 "탄핵을 당하더라도 스스로 물러나는 일은 없다"고 버텼다. 이에 응답이라도 하듯 촛불은 두 배인 200만으로 불어났다. 이후 박근혜의 '질서 있는 퇴진론'이 고개를 들었으나 촛불시민의 화만 돋웠다. 12월 3일에는 사상 최대의 232만의 촛불이 타올랐다. 촛불은 흔들리는 정치권에 '박근혜 즉각 탄핵'을 명령했고, 2016년 12월 9일 마침내 국회 탄핵안이 가결됐다.

"주문, 피청구인 대통령 박근혜를 파면한다."

국회의 탄핵 결정이 내려진지 3개월 만인 2017년 3월 10일, 헌법재판소가 재판관 전원일치로 박근혜 대통령을 파면했다. 그러나 박근혜를 권좌에서 끌어내린 진짜 주역은 국회도 헌법재판소도 아닌, 광장의 촛불과 일부 언론이었다. JTBC, 한겨레, 경향 등은 고비 고비마다 박근혜와 비선들의 국정농단과 거짓말을 확인보도 함으로써 촛불시민들에게 힘과 용기를 심어주었다. 뉴스타파, 국민TV, 오마이뉴스, 미디어오늘, 프레시안 등 인터넷 대안언론들 또한 권부의 확성기가 된 공영방송과 족벌언론의 여론 조작을 막아내는데 힘을 보탰다. 그렇게 해서 촛불은 주말마다 10만에서 100만, 100만에서 200만으로 불어났다.

대통령 탄핵 이후에도 족벌언론은 편파 왜곡을 일삼았고, 거짓 주장과 가짜뉴스를 여과 없이 전파했다. 박근혜 보위대인 태극기부대의 준동도 끊이질 않았다. 대선 국면으로 전환되면서 족벌언론은 '수구'의 본성을 본격적으로 드러냈다. 동아일보는 박근혜에 대한 '불구속 수사'를 촉구했고, 조선일보는 "전직 대통령에 대한 예우를 갖추라"고 훈계했다. KBS, MBC, YTN, 연합뉴스 등 공영방송사와 통신사는 진실과 정의를 외면한 채 '촛불과 태극기부대의 이념대결'로 몰아갔다.

이러한 언론 현실로는 촛불이 갈망했던 적폐 청산과 대한민국의 미래는 요원한 일이었다.

2017년 5월 9일 문재인 정부 출범 후, 이명박 박근혜 정권 하에서 처절하게 망가진 공영방송을 복원해야 한다는 움직임이 다시 일었다. 전국언론노동조합, 자유언론실천재단, 동아투위, 민주언론시민연합, 새언론포럼, 언론연대, 언론소비자주권행동 등 240여 시민사회단체는 'KBS·MBC정상화시민행동'(시민행동)을 발족했다. 시민행동은 7월 21일부터 매주 금요일 저녁 시민문화제를 개최하는 등 공영방송정상화를 촉구하는 다양한 활동을 펼쳤다. 시민행동은 공영방송을 몰락시킨 '주범'으로 박근혜 정권의 방송장악에 부역했던 공영방송의 이사들을 지목하고 방송통신위원회에 이들의 파면을 촉구하는 '시민청원서'를 제출했다.

2017년 공영방송 구성원들의 파업투쟁이 다시 시작되고, 시민사회의 공영방송 정상화 촉구 움직임이 거세지자, 지난 정권에 부역했던 공영방송의 이사들이 사퇴하기 시작했다. 이후 새롭게 구성된 방송문화진흥회(방문진)와 KBS이사회는 공개적이고 투명한 절차를 밟아 MBC와 KBS의 사장을 새로 임명했다. 사장 선임 과정에서 정치권의 개입은 없었고 개입할 여지도 없었다.

언론자유는 모든 자유를
자유롭게 한다

헌정사를 돌이켜보면 독재 권력은 하나같이 불행한 최후를 맞았다. 이승만은 국민의 비난 속에 고국에서 쫓겨나 망명지에서 쓸쓸히 생을 마감했다. 박정희는 직속 부하의 총탄에 무참히 살해됐다. 전두환, 노태우, 이명박, 박근혜는 감옥에 갔다. 그 비극의 역사 속에는 항상 언론의 문제가 도사리고 있었다. 독재자는 언론을 장악하려 했다. 거기에는 늘 부도덕한 관료가 있었고, 영달을 꿈꾸는 부역 언론인이 있었다. 독재자와 유착되어 권력을 탐닉하다가 위기에 처하면 갈아치우는 하이에나 언론이 있었다. 그러한 역사는 변함없이 반복됐다.

언론환경이 이처럼 무도하고 위험스러워진 데는 단 한 번

도 부역언론에 대한 청산의 역사가 없었기 때문이다. 일제 강점기에 부화한 친일족벌언론들은 해방 이후에도 청산은커녕 독재시대를 거치며 급성장했다. 친일족벌언론은 독재정권과 유착해 민주주의를 억압했고 안보상업주의로 부를 축적했다. '종북', '좌파', '빨갱이' 따위의 색깔 공세로 사회 분열을 획책해온 친일족벌언론은 이제 스스로 정권을 창출할 수도 있고 퇴출시킬 수도 있는 무소불위의 권력을 자처하기에 이르렀다.

박근혜를 끌어내린 광장의 촛불시민들은 "언론도 공범"이라고 외쳤다. 그러나 더 정확하게 표현한다면, 족벌언론은 '공범'이 아니라, 일제 강점기부터 100여 년 동안 변신을 거듭하면서 수탈의 역사를 지속시켜온 적폐의 '주범'이었다. 그래서 적폐 청산의 첫 번째 단계는 친일족벌언론과 기회주의 부역 언론인들을 청산하는 일부터 시작되어야 한다.

3.1운동 후 100년이 된 2019년의 대한민국은 표현의 자유가 넘쳐나는 세상이다. 그 속에서 가짜뉴스와 근거 없는 주장들이 횡행하고 있다. 과거에도 유언비어 통신은 있었지만 이제 입에서 입으로 전해지는 뜬소문은 신문이나 TV처럼 언론 보도의 형식을 띠고 전파되어 무엇이 진실인지 구분하기 어렵다. 사실이 아닌 것을 사실인양 주장하고, 한 조각의 사실로 전체를 규정하며, 관련성 없는 사실의 조각들을 짜깁기 해

진실인 양 포장하는 오늘의 언론 현실은 우리 사회를 분열과 혼돈으로 몰아가고 있다.

언론의 자유는 모든 자유를 자유롭게 한다. 그러나 거짓을 말할 수 있는 자유를 자유의 이름으로 용인할 수는 없다. 이 혼돈의 시대에 언론운동의 역할은 무엇인가. 밀턴의 경구대로 허위와 왜곡과 날조의 언어들이 '사상의 자유시장'에서 걸러지도록 하기 위한 전략적 언론운동을 적극적으로 펴나갈 시점이다.

혹자는 "언제나 투쟁이 없는 세상이 될 것인가"라고 묻는다. 그러나 인간의 역사가 항상 목가적인 것만은 아니었다. 투쟁과 운동의 역사는 어느 시대, 어느 곳에서나 존재했고 앞으로도 존재할 것이다. 그것은 보다 나은 세상을 꿈꾸는 사람들의 몫이며 그들이 있기에 역사는 발전한다.

참고
문헌

김종철(2013), 「폭력의 자유」, ㈜참언론 시사IN북

동아자유언론수호투쟁위원회(2005), 「자유언론」 해담솔

민주언론시민연합(2017), 「보도지침 1986 그리고 2016」, 도서출판 두레

새언론포럼(2008), 「현장기록, 방송노조 민주화운동 20년」 커뮤니케이션북스(주)

새언론포럼(2009), 「현장기록, 신문노조 민주화운동 20년」 커뮤니케이션북스(주)

원희복(2004), 「조용수와 민족일보」, 도서출판새누리

5.18기념재단(2014), 「5.18민주화운동과 언론투쟁」, 도서출판 심미안

Kim, Sae-Eun. "Journalism History: Korea." *In Media History and the Foundations of Media Studies. Edited by John Nerone. Vol. 1 of The International Encyclopedia of Media Studies*, First Edition. Edited by Angharad N. Valdivia. Blackwell Publishing, 2013.

"A Reconstruction of Korean Journalism History through Dismissed Journalists' Career and Life." *Ŏllon'gwa sahoe* 18, No. 4 (2010): 158–208.